SURVIVING ALIEN CONTACT AND WARFARE

ALIEN MYTHS AND FACTS

SEAN T. PAGE

ROSEN
PUBLISHING®

THIS EDITION PUBLISHED IN 2017 BY

THE ROSEN PUBLISHING GROUP, INC.
29 EAST 21ST STREET
NEW YORK, NY 10010

LIBRARY OF CONGRESS CATALOGING-IN-PUBLICATION DATA

NAMES: PAGE, SEAN T., AUTHOR.
TITLE: ALIEN MYTHS AND FACTS / SEAN T. PAGE.
OTHER TITLES: ALIEN INVASION MANUAL
DESCRIPTION: NEW YORK, NY : ROSEN PUBLISHING GROUP, INC., [2017] | SERIES: SURVIVING ALIEN CONTACT AND WARFARE | INCLUDES BIBLIOGRAPHICAL REFERENCES AND INDEX.
IDENTIFIERS: LCCN 2016035781| ISBN 9781499465235 (LIBRARY BOUND) | ISBN 9781499465228 (6 PACK) | ISBN 9781499465211 (PBK.)
SUBJECTS: LCSH: EXTRATERRESTRIAL BEINGS. | HUMAN-ALIEN ENCOUNTERS. | SURVIVAL.
CLASSIFICATION: LCC BF2050 .P328 2017 | DDC 001.942--DC23
LC RECORD AVAILABLE AT HTTPS://LCCN.LOC.GOV/2016035781

MANUFACTURED IN CHINA

ORIGINALLY PUBLISHED IN ENGLISH BY HAYNES PUBLISHING UNDER THE TITLE: *ALIEN INVASION MANUAL* © SEAN T. PAGE 2014.

CONTENTS

CLASSIFIED INFORMATION

MINISTRY OF ALIEN DEFENSE · DEFENDING EARTH FOR HUMANITY ·

DON'T PANIC

YOU MUST READ THE FOLLOWING BEFORE CONTINUING

In the first decades of the 21st century, the volume of the radio and television transmissions we send out into the universe has expanded exponentially. You can add to this the various objects we've fired into space over the years, including NASA's Voyager probe, which was launched almost 40 years ago and has just entered interstellar space, heading for the mysterious Oort cloud. But can we be sure whoever is out there is friendly?

These activities of ours are like sending an open invitation to every other life form in the blackness of space. And the invitation reads, "Please come and take my planet!" Not surprisingly, we have already attracted interest from aliens and we know of at least four extraterrestrial species who are either intervening in human affairs or preparing invasion plans against us. The alien threat to Earth is no longer science fiction – it's science fact!

This manual is designed to provide you with the latest scientific insight and intelligence on aliens and their plans to take over our planet. This information will ensure that you're equipped not only to resist abductions, invasive implants and survive an alien invasion, but also to lead a human fight-back and even take the war to the alien home world.

Published by the Ministry of Alien Defense in London, this volume calls on a vast wealth of knowledge and experience, from access to secret US Air Force UFO files and abduction case studies to evidence from the latest alien vehicle crash site in China and top-secret plans for the creation of a united Earth defense force. The United Nations Office for Earth Defense has been heavily involved in ensuring that the facts and figures within this volume are the best we have. Even if you count yourself as a sceptic, please do read on as we present here, for the first time, all information on the known species that may soon invade our planet.

This manual is not designed for astronauts, boffins or eggheads. It's for everyone. In true Haynes style, we aim to demonstrate how with the right knowledge, training and the largest available roll of aluminium foil, the concerned citizen can really hit ET where it hurts. You can protect your home and family from mind-bending abductions, you can ensure that you remain free of any sinister implants, and you can determine which shape-shifting lizards are working to take over society.

But for now, put on your tin-foil hat and read on. A strange and sometimes frightening world is about to open up for you.

Sean T. Page
Ministry of Alien Defense, London

ALIENS – FACT OR FICTION?

This volume is about the interference of alien life in human affairs. This could be friendly – we certainly hope so. But most experts agree that an alien presence is more likely to be hostile, ranging from spying and abductions to a full-scale invasion of Earth.

Before even planning for an alien invasion, it's important that you are up to date with all the facts. Perhaps you don't believe in life on other worlds, or that aliens would be interested in taking over our planet? Perhaps you think all these UFO and abduction stories are hoaxes? Well, read on. In this section we'll survey the published evidence to date and not only prove that aliens exist but that governments know about their existence.

 ARE WE ALONE?

Keep watching the skies!

The short answer is "no." This is the one area on which virtually every scientist agrees. Where do we start?

▶ We exist in a dodecahedron-shaped universe that's at least 150 billion light years wide – that's big. But to show how little we know about it, around 75% of the energy in the universe is made up of so-called "dark energy" and we don't have much of a clue what that is.

▶ The universe is populated by billions of galaxies, some spiral-shaped, some elliptical and some in the shapes of amusing vegetables. Basically, there are loads of them!

▶ Since 2008 scientists working at United Nations Office for Earth Defense observatories have confirmed the existence of hundreds of Earth-like planets – and these are just the ones we can see. More theoretical studies have estimated that there are around 12,000 alien civilizations in our galaxy alone.

▶ As you'll discover as you read through this book, the final proof that we're not alone is the sheer number of alien sightings, abductions, implants and fiendish invasion plans being noted across the world every day – as well as the several ships, bodies and live extraterrestrials that have been seized by Earth's various security agencies.

▶ To date, the world has comprehensive data on five known alien species in the universe, with fragmentary evidence suggesting the existence of over a hundred more. Out of these five, four appear to have hostile intentions towards humanity and our planet.

ALIENS – FACT OR FICTION?
DO YOU BELIEVE?

In a recent survey by the International Space Agency, over 50% of people reported that they had either experienced an alien encounter or firmly believed in their existence.

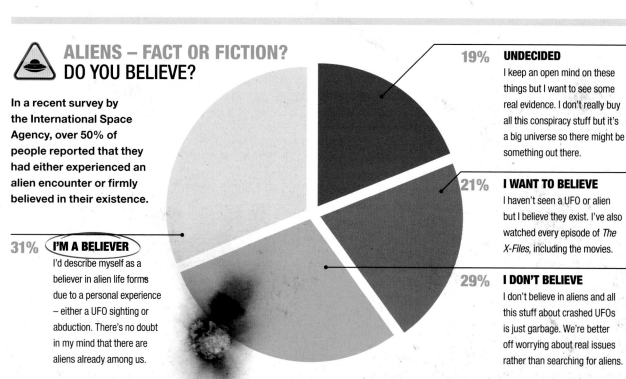

19% UNDECIDED
I keep an open mind on these things but I want to see some real evidence. I don't really buy all this conspiracy stuff but it's a big universe so there might be something out there.

21% I WANT TO BELIEVE
I haven't seen a UFO or alien but I believe they exist. I've also watched every episode of *The X-Files*, including the movies.

29% I DON'T BELIEVE
I don't believe in aliens and all this stuff about crashed UFOs is just garbage. We're better off worrying about real issues rather than searching for aliens.

31% I'M A BELIEVER
I'd describe myself as a believer in alien life forms due to a personal experience – either a UFO sighting or abduction. There's no doubt in my mind that there are aliens already among us.

SURVEY OF 1,598 PEOPLE, MARCH 2014

 MINISTRY OF ALIEN DEFENSE

▶ DO YOU BELIEVE IN ALIENS?

Popular perception can only ever tell half of the story. Here at the Ministry of Alien Defense our stock-in-trade is hard facts. We have literally hundreds of case files, eyewitness accounts and alien artifacts that prove beyond all doubt not only that aliens exist in the universe but that they have also visited Earth many times. And, before you get a picture of us believers as a sectarian lunatic fringe, here's a list of famous people in history and what they have personally experienced or stated about extraterrestrials. Browse through these quotes from military leaders, politicians and even former presidents. Remember, if you already believe, you're clearly not alone!

"I CAN ASSURE YOU THAT FLYING SAUCERS, GIVEN THAT THEY EXIST, ARE NOT CONSTRUCTED BY ANY POWER ON EARTH."

PRESIDENT HARRY S. TRUMAN
33RD PRESIDENT OF THE UNITED STATES, 1950

"IF I BECOME PRESIDENT, I'LL MAKE EVERY PIECE OF INFORMATION THIS COUNTRY HAS ABOUT UFO SIGHTINGS AVAILABLE TO THE PUBLIC AND SCIENTISTS. I AM CONVINCED THAT UFOs EXIST BECAUSE I HAVE SEEN ONE."

PRESIDENT JIMMY CARTER
DURING HIS PRESIDENTIAL CAMPAIGN, 1969

"THE PEOPLE'S REPUBLIC OF CHINA IS FULLY AWARE OF THE RISKS POSED BY THE ALIEN THREAT AND HAVE ACTED TO COUNTER THESE THREATS BOTH ON EARTH AND IN SPACE."

GENERAL WANG LI-CHA
MILITARY LIAISON TO UNITED NATIONS IN NEW YORK, 2009

"I BELIEVE THAT THESE EXTRATERRESTRIAL VEHICLES AND THEIR CREWS ARE VISITING THIS PLANET FROM OTHER PLANETS... MOST ASTRONAUTS WERE RELUCTANT TO DISCUSS UFOs. I DID HAVE OCCASION IN 1951 TO HAVE TWO DAYS OF OBSERVATION OF MANY FLIGHTS OF THEM, OF DIFFERENT SIZES, FLYING IN FIGHTER FORMATION, GENERALLY FROM EAST TO WEST OVER EUROPE."

MAJOR GORDON COOPER
NASA ASTRONAUT TO THE UNITED NATIONS, 1978

"THE UNITED STATES MILITARY ARE PREPARING WEAPONS THAT COULD BE USED AGAINST THE ALIENS, AND THEY COULD GET US INTO AN INTERGALACTIC WAR WITHOUT US EVER HAVING ANY WARNING... THE BUSH ADMINISTRATION HAS FINALLY AGREED TO LET THE MILITARY BUILD A FORWARD BASE ON THE MOON, WHICH WILL PUT THEM IN A BETTER POSITION TO KEEP TRACK OF THE GOINGS AND COMINGS OF THE VISITORS FROM SPACE, AND TO SHOOT AT THEM, IF THEY SO DECIDE."

PAUL THEODORE HELLYER
FORMER SENIOR MINISTER, CANADIAN PARLIAMENT, 2005

"THE NEXT WAR WILL BE AN INTERPLANETARY WAR. THE NATIONS MUST SOME DAY MAKE A COMMON FRONT AGAINST ATTACK BY PEOPLE FROM OTHER PLANETS."

DOUGLAS MACARTHUR
FORMER FIVE-STAR GENERAL OF THE US ARMY, 1955

"THE NUMBER OF PLANETS IN OUR GALAXY ON WHICH A TECHNOLOGICAL CIVILIZATION IS NOW IN BEING IS ROUGHLY 530,000."

ISAAC ASIMOV
EXTRATERRESTRIAL CIVILIZATIONS, 1980

"I'VE BEEN CONVINCED FOR A LONG TIME THAT THE FLYING SAUCERS ARE INTERPLANETARY. WE ARE BEING WATCHED BY BEINGS FROM OUTER SPACE."

ALBERT M. CHOP
DEPUTY PUBLIC RELATIONS DIRECTOR, NASA, 1965

"OF COURSE THE FLYING SAUCERS ARE REAL, AND THEY ARE INTERPLANETARY."

AIR CHIEF MARSHAL LORD DOWDING
CHIEF OF THE ROYAL AIR FORCE DURING WORLD WAR II, 1954

"WITH OUR OBSESSION WITH ANTAGONISMS OF THE MOMENT, WE OFTEN FORGET HOW MUCH UNITES ALL THE MEMBERS OF HUMANITY. I OCCASIONALLY THINK HOW QUICKLY OUR DIFFERENCES, WORLDWIDE, WOULD VANISH IF WE WERE FACING AN ALIEN THREAT FROM OUTSIDE THIS WORLD."

PRESIDENT RONALD REAGAN
40TH PRESIDENT OF THE UNITED STATES, 1988

ALIENS – FACT OR FICTION?

THE ALIEN FOOTPRINT ON EARTH

Even if you're prepared to believe the vast weight of scientific evidence about life in other parts of the universe, you may still be sceptical as to whether aliens would ever make it to our isolated part of our very nondescript spiral galaxy. We'll take an in-depth look at alien motivation shortly, but for the moment consider these facts about UFO sightings and alien abductions.

UFO SIGHTINGS

Before the creation of the Ministry of Alien Defense in 1981, UFO sightings were collected by the RAF but other government agencies such as the Department for War and the National Health Service also gathered data separately, making it very difficult to consolidate an overall picture of sightings in the UK.

Since the creation of the Ministry hotline in 1989, things have thankfully become much clearer and we can now confirm some statistics concerning the number of people in the UK and Ireland who have reported UFO sightings.

Of course, these figures need to be read carefully. For example, these are "verified reports," which means that they've been investigated by the "Men in Black" and deemed "viable sightings." Investigating agencies tend to dismiss fanciful accounts or those from unreliable sources. However, it's important to consider that many of these may be sightings of the same alien ship. For instance, in 2009 a gray saucer entered UK airspace and flew the length of the country. Not surprisingly, the Ministry was bombarded with accounts of the vessel, with witnesses corroborating each other's stories with sketches of the ship and comments regarding its slow speed.

Our statistics confirm that the level of alien activity over the UK has certainly increased. Even if we allow for some inaccuracy in reporting, many other countries are experiencing the same trend. Basically, there are more and more alien craft visiting our planet and this is further supported by a disturbing growth in the number of abductions.

ALIENS – FACT OR FICTION?
RECORDED UFO SIGHTINGS

The following statistics are the UK's official figures on UFO sightings and include reports made by the RAF and other armed forces as well as members of the public.

Year	Sightings
1990	10,233
1995	12,666
2000	13,599
2005	16,322
2010	18,000
2017	22,000 +

> **IN MILITARY TERMS, IT WOULD SEEM THAT WE ARE BEING ASSESSED AND STUDIED. OUR ANALYSIS HAS SHOWN AN UNCOMFORTABLE CORRELATION BETWEEN UFO SIGHTINGS AND KEY MILITARY AND INFRASTRUCTURE INSTALLATIONS. LOOKING AT IT FROM A COLD AND STRATEGIC VIEWPOINT, OUR CAPABILITIES ARE BEING EXAMINED AND CATALOGUED BY FORCES FROM BEYOND OUR SPACE.**
> **GENERAL WILHELM FOKKER, EU DEFENSE ADVISER, 2008**

This is what I saw over the school in 1995

DATA TAKEN FROM MINISTRY OF ALIEN DEFENSE RECORDS 1989-2014

ALIEN ABDUCTIONS

As with UFO sightings, only recently have we begun to gather statistics on what's now recognized to be a worldwide phenomenon – alien abduction. This is the taking of a human against his or her will to meet some kind of alien need, typically medical research. The number of people disappearing worldwide is at an all-time high. There's no single database, but the USA, Japan, and Europe keep the best statistics.

▶ According to the charity Missing Persons, over 20,000 Britons vanish every year.

▶ In the USA, some 2,300 people vanish every day – there's no trace and they're never seen again. This excludes those who return within 48 hours of going missing.

▶ In Japan, since 2001, over 4,000,000 people have been reported to the police as missing.

▶ Over 100,000 people globally say they've been implanted with alien tracking devices or "implants" – some of them are probably crazy, but all of them?

Some people, of course, change their identities, start a new life, fall down a well or just jump in the sea when their favorite sci-fi show is cancelled, but we're still looking at millions of people every year going missing and the evidence increasingly suggests that they're being taken by beings from beyond this Earth. And these reports aren't just restricted to Europe, North America, and Japan. In 2005, General Wang Li-Cha of the People's Red Army in China reportedly told a US counterpart that no less than 42% of the Chinese cyber-defense budget was allocated to combating what he termed "the saucer disappearances" and "reptilian conspiracies." According to Pentagon sources, the General reported that over 93,000 people had been taken by aliens in 2004 alone in the People's Republic of China and that it was on the agenda of the party, which considered the issue a threat to the nation.

> SINCE THE COLLAPSE OF THE US TREATY WITH THE GRAYS IN 1980, IT'S BECOME OPEN SEASON ON EARTH, WITH THE NUMBER OF ABDUCTIONS GOING THROUGH THE ROOF. IF WE WERE HONEST WITH THE PUBLIC, WE'D HAVE TO SAY THAT WE'RE CURRENTLY POWERLESS TO STOP THESE SHIPS ENTERING OUR AIRSPACE AND KIDNAPPING CITIZENS AT WILL.
> **MINISTRY OF DEFENSE BRIEFING, WHITEHALL, 2014**

▶ SO WHY NOW?

If aliens have been around for so many years, how is it that we're only now just beginning to see the scope and threat of extraterrestrial intervention on our planet? Why didn't they just invade when we were at a much lower level of development?

It's a good question and in truth no one is 100% sure. We know that aliens have attempted interventions on Earth before and some of these will be explored in later chapters. However, there are several factors in the past few decades that have made us a far more viable prospect for invasion.

MORE NOISE

Our noise level in the universe has greatly increased in the past 50 years – we've sent out into space everything from deep-space probes with our image and location to episodes of all the idiotic TV shows that have ever been made.

Add to this our rudimentary attempts at space travel and the creation and use of nuclear weapons, and you can see that our activities cannot have gone unnoticed to species outside our solar system.

SEIZE THE DAY

The requirements of some potential invaders have changed. For example, the Grays have tried some form of dialogue with humanity to support their need for vast quantities of DNA and biomatter, but for them talking simply hasn't delivered what they need. For others, such as the Draconians and Little Green Men, perhaps they see the present as the opportune time to invade – before we develop any further.

ALIENS – FACT OR FICTION?

GREAT ALIEN MYTHS

By now you should be convinced that there are envious alien eyes watching our planet very closely and working on their invasion plans. However, this doesn't mean that every negative thing happening on Earth is down to extraterrestrial visitors. In this section we debunk some of the widely held misconceptions about aliens. It's vital that we all focus on our real objective, which is to prevent a takeover of Earth by alien forces rather than spend months trying to prove that a weird circle in the cornfields of Wiltshire was caused by a rogue X-wing fighter.

Any search on the internet will uncover hundreds of myths relating to alien intervention on Earth. While there's some truth hidden among the many web pages of fiction, it's often hard to tell one from the other. This section, therefore, will focus on the most pervasive myths around extraterrestrials – we'll leave out the most fantastical stuff. We should also inject a note of caution: in this field what can at first sound bizarre may one day turn out to be the truth. So here's what we know for sure – so far!

MYTH 1
ALIENS ARE CAUSING GLOBAL CLIMATE CHANGE

Some people say that Earth is getting hotter, others that it's getting colder. The reptiles prefer it warm, so they must be heating up the planet; the Grays like it cool, so it must be them cooling it down. Nothing divides alien watchers and conspiracy theorists more than the controversy of climate change. There's no doubt that species such as the Draconians would prefer a warmer Earth and there's some evidence that they're linked to some of the world's biggest CO_2 polluting companies. As for other species, we have no real proof that they're purposely manipulating our environment. This doesn't mean that species such as the Little Green Men won't get busy "terra-forming" once they actually invade, but for the moment the quantity of greenhouse gases we're pumping into the Earth's atmosphere is all our own work.

MYTH 2
ALIENS ARE RESPONSIBLE FOR CROP CIRCLES

Crop circles are the biggest hoax in alien investigations and more words have been wasted on them than on, for example, practical military plans for the defense of our planet. At a rough count, there are over 4,000 books on the subject, with theories ranging from how they're created by gods to suggestions that they're messages from aliens trying to make contact. In the very real world of alien defense, the only "crop circles" we recognize are the burn marks left by a Gray saucer. Whenever these ships or other space vessels land on the planet, they leave indentations, burns or scorch marks, and, yes, crushed crops. Sometimes they're left in circular patterns, sometimes not. But we have no evidence that any species is trying to make contact by leaving odd shapes in our countryside.

ALIENS – FACT OR FICTION?
THE RISE OF REALITY TV

It may seem strange to readers that while classic TV series such as *Firefly* are cancelled, reality shows with their "follow-a-nobody" formula are regularly getting into their fifth series. But does this rapid expansion of lousy TV really mean that the cold, clammy hand of the alien invader is at work in TV studios? The simple answer is that we don't know. Media is certainly a useful way to reach the mass populace and billions of people around the world have access to TV, but we have no evidence at the moment that aliens are working to "dumb down" our TV programs and in the process dumbing down the IQ of the general populace. Aliens would be better off spending their time damaging computer, engineering, math, and science education in schools and colleges, for these are the disciplines we need to meet the technological challenges that lie ahead.

> **IT HAS BEEN ESTIMATED THAT THE AVERAGE ADULT WILL LOSE ONE IQ POINT FOR EVERY 20 HOURS OF REALITY TV WATCHED. THIS INCREASES TO TWO IQ POINTS IF THE SHOW INVOLVES A PHONE VOTE.**
> **WASHINGTON INSTITUTE OF EMPIRICAL RESEARCH**

MYTH 3
NEW-AGE CULTS ARE A GOOD WAY TO MEET ALIENS

There are several prominent quasi-religious organizations around the world that cite contact with extraterrestrials as one of their "membership benefits." Invariably, any contact ends up costing a fortune and several of these cults are now thriving, offering everything from a free half-consultation with a Gray to guaranteed rescues in an alien ship when the world ends. Alien visitors have had contact from time to time with religious leaders in the past but most of this contact by far has been through the Nordics via Buddhist monks in Tibet and India. While other alien species struggle to get their very different minds around human religion, the Nordics have engaged in open dialogue with those they perceive as enlightened. This doesn't extend to the locally produced monthly DVDs for just $15.99 on subscription.

MYTH 4
SO, WHAT'S GOING ON WITH THE BEES?

There has been a suspected link between aliens and bees since the 1970s and many conspiracy theorists have pointed to the potentially disastrous collapse in pollinator numbers as evidence of an alien conspiracy at work. The often-cited hypothesis is that the Grays have manipulated bee DNA in an effort to either spread "rogue DNA" throughout our ecosystem or as part of their own DNA-splicing trials. Wilder theories suggest that alien invaders are attacking our ecosystem by stealth, by destroying some of the key pillars of nature such as pollination. The TV series ████████ played very much on the fear that aliens were experimenting with bees. Those patient enough to follow this long-running series were further confused when it linked bees with a plan to spread a virus among the human population.

ALIENS – FACT OR FICTION?

THE UK PERSPECTIVE

Although the facts contained in this volume have been gathered from international sources, the Ministry of Alien Defense (MAD) in London is charged with protecting the UK population and airspace from the extraterrestrial threat. The office was created in 1981 following events in the USA; prior to this alien threats had been managed and investigated by the RAF. The MAD now fields a force of over 200 managers and 50 Men in Black investigation teams. The Extraterrestrial Security Act 1979 defines our role as being:

> **THE PROTECTION OF NATIONAL SECURITY AND, IN PARTICULAR, ITS PROTECTION AGAINST THREATS FROM ABDUCTION, IMPLANTS, AND LIVESTOCK MUTILATION, FROM THE ACTIVITIES OF AGENTS OF ALIEN POWERS, AND FROM ACTIONS INTENDED TO UNDERMINE PARLIAMENTARY DEMOCRACY BY POLITICAL, INDUSTRIAL, OR VIOLENT MEANS.**
> **THE EXTRATERRESTRIAL SECURITY ACT**

IN PURSUING THE ROLE SET OUT BY THE ACT, THE CORPORATE AIMS OF THE MINISTRY OF ALIEN DEFENSE ARE:

▶ Frustrate alien intervention.

▶ Prevent damage to the UK from alien espionage and other covert alien activity.

▶ Foster the procurement of alien material, technology, or expertise relating to weapons or propulsion.

▶ Watch out for new or re-emerging types of alien threats, particularly around cloning.

▶ Protect Government's sensitive information and assets, and the Critical National Infrastructure (CNI).

▶ Assist the Secret Intelligence Service (SIS) and the Government Communications Headquarters (GCHQ) in the discharge of their statutory functions.

▶ Build resilience to a possible invasion from outer space and management of the UK's Men in Black resources.

▶ Work with the United Nations Office for Earth Defense.

ALIENS – FACT OR FICTION?
THE UK'S MEN IN BLACK

Tales of UFO witnesses and abductees being visited by "Men in Black" date back as far as the 1830s in the USA. They have often been seen as part of some sinister plot by the government to silence people on the alien threat to Earth or, worse still, as part of the extraterrestrial invasion itself. However, for the Men in Black operating in the UK today, nothing could be further from the truth.

EYEWITNESS ACCOUNT

Peggy Moore, 89, from Grasslands Nursing Home has been abducted over 100 times in her lifetime. She's seen how the Men in Black have changed their approach over the years.

> **THE GRILLING THE AGENTS GAVE ME WHEN I RETURNED WAS WORSE THAN THE ABDUCTION ITSELF. THEY ASKED ALL KINDS OF QUESTIONS, BANGING THE TABLE WHEN I DIDN'T ANSWER MUCH. AND, WOE BETIDE IF YOU DIDN'T REPORT IT. NOW IT'S DIFFERENT. YOU CAN BOOK AN APPOINTMENT WITH THEM ONLINE AND THEY'RE VERY POLITE.**
> **PEGGY MOORE, 100+ ALIEN ABDUCTIONS**

FACTS ABOUT MEN IN BLACK UNITS IN THE UK

▶ A Men in Black unit is typically made up of 2–3 special agents, with one being office-based at any one time.

▶ The term "Men in Black" is no longer used within the Ministry of Alien Defense, the teams being referred to as Extraterrestrial Investigation Units (ETIU).

▶ Over 54% of Men in Black are in fact female and very few agents actually wear black. In addition, few wear sunglasses due to health and safety concerns.

▶ Recruitment of Men in Black is generally via other UK, Irish, American, or Commonwealth security agencies.

▶ Men in Black are officially categorized as "civil servants." Their role sounds exciting – in 2016 they filed over 6,000 UFO sighting and abduction reports – but they are in fact as skilled in paperwork as they are with ray guns!

▶ Like MI5 and MI6 agents, investigators working for the Ministry of Alien Defense carry the same authority in law as a senior police inspector. In other words, they have an official badge that enables them to enter any location where they have suspicions that a "crime" is taking place. Most are licensed to carry firearms or other "high-tech" weapons.

ARE YOU INTERESTED IN *REALLY* SAVING THE PLANET?

M. A.D.

THEN YOU SHOULD JOIN THE MINISTRY OF ALIEN DEFENSE

GET INVOLVED • SAVE THE WORLD • SAVE HUMANITY

CURRENT VACANCIES
▶ **Operational Infrastructure Engineers**
▶ **Binary code experts**
▶ **Nosy-parkers**

Joining one of our frontline Extraterrestrial Investigation Units is a perfect way to help save the planet from the unwelcome attention of aliens. Whatever your role, you can expect your caseload to be diverse and ever-changing. One day you could be helping to install an aluminium cover to the home of a multiple abduction victim, the next you might be working with other agents on a real UFO crash site.

TIME FOR A CHANGE?
There's plenty of scope for career development and the agency particularly welcomes those who are interested in conspiracy theories or who are regularly regarded as being "a bit paranoid." As we say here in the agency, "Just because you're paranoid, it doesn't mean they're not out to get you!" No previous alien-busting experience required and positions attract an extensive benefits package including:

▶ **A competitive salary**
▶ **The occasional "excursion" to Area 51**
▶ **A lifetime's supply of aluminium foil**

ADVICE FOR APPLICANTS
Owing to the sensitivity of our work, we don't publicly disclose the identities of our staff. Discretion is vital. You shouldn't discuss your application with anyone other than your partner or a close family member. You should also make them aware of the importance of discretion. Mostly they'll just think you're nuts as few of the population even know we exist.

If you're a friendly alien already on Earth, then please email the Ministry for further information. The Ministry is an equal opportunity employer for all species.

ALIEN KNOWLEDGE 101

If you've read this far, you should now be convinced of the real threat to our planet. There are aliens out there – fact. Tens of thousands of humans are being abducted every year – fact. Our planet is woefully unprepared to face any invasion – fact.

For those new to these facts, it can all be a bit overwhelming. One immediately starts thinking about sending cash to NASA or wearing a tinfoil hat when outdoors. But the first step to defending our planet is knowledge.

The term "alien" describes every species other than humanity but this group is far from homogenous, with different physiology, social structure, and even chemical make-up. In fact, we now know that there are millions of different species out there – currently the Ministry of Alien Defense recognizes around <u>300 different life forms and they all have different drivers, motives, and game plans.</u>

DRIVERS FOR INVASION

Assessing alien drivers for invasion is a bit like asking why humans fight wars on Earth – in reality it's a complex mix of greed, jealousy, empire building, scientific curiosity, and even species eradication. Every alien species out there will have its own unique needs and pressures.

Over the years organizations have used various descriptions to categorize the invasion motives of aliens – terms include destroyers, imperial powers, scavengers, re-locators, raiders, and crusaders. All of this caused significant confusion among the alien-watching community, so in 2006 the Ministry of Alien Defense started working with the United Nations Organization for Earth Defense on a unified classification of alien invasion motives. Was that meeting as interesting as it sounds? The outcomes are presented on the facing page.

ALIEN KNOWLEDGE 101
WHY HAVE YOU COME TO EARTH?

The website wiki-alieninvasion.com claims that 42 alien ships have crashed on Earth since 1912, leaving 17 survivors representing at least four different species. By hacking into top-secret documents around the world, the website claims that it can reveal the answer to the real question we want to ask – why have you come to Earth?

*Do not trust wiki-alieninvasion.com
— the founder is currently sheltering in the Venezuelan embassy after clocking up hundreds of unpaid parking tickets*

SHOULD WE BELIEVE THIS SURVEY?

Well, it's the only one of its kind ever attempted and although we cannot validate the sources, the survey seems to suggest that in the past we had more positive interactions with alien species – and we do know that since the 1980s we have had very little positive communication with alien species. This suggests that those species that do "want to get to know us" have been driven away or have left the scene, leaving us open to the more hostile varieties. The results have been moderated against a scale as communication has not always been in an Earth language and not all aliens could answer the question.

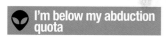 It sounded like fun

I'm below my abduction quota

We bring great advances in science and medicine

We find your planet and species of interest and have come to observe

$$x = (-1)^n \arcsin \frac{1}{2} + \pi n = (-1)^n \frac{\pi}{6}$$

$$x = \pm \arccos \frac{\sqrt{2}}{2} + 2\pi n = \pm \frac{\pi}{4} + 2\pi$$

$$x = \arctan \sqrt{3} + \pi n = \frac{\pi}{3} + \pi n_{\sin 2}$$

We need more food so have come to raid your planet for resources

 To rid the Earth of the human vermin. Your very existence is offensive to my species!

SOURCE: VARIOUS NATIONAL GOVERNMENT RECORDS AND THE WASHINGTON MEMORANDUM, VOL. IX

▶ ALIEN MOTIVATION MATRIX

In 2008 the United Nations Organization for Earth Defense agreed an Alien Motivation Matrix that's now used world-wide to help develop plans to manage and combat any hostile alien intervention on Earth or within our solar system.

The Matrix is far from perfect and it's immediately clear how these basic categories can overlap and change over time. They must also be considered alongside the capacity of an alien species to invade Earth. For example, a species limited to a few hundred beings will be unlikely to want to risk a ground offensive on the planet and, despite its advanced technology, may not be able to complete a takeover, preferring instead to use more subtle means.

CLASSIFICATION	KEY FEATURES, VECTORS & METHODS	EXAMPLES FROM KNOWN SPECIES
1 OBSERVERS	Very low probability of hostile intervention. Possible avoidance of contact altogether. May be operating under a *Star Trek* type "prime directive" of non-intervention. There's a risk that this category could move into a judgement phase in which assessment is made of humanity's right to exist.	▶ **The Nordics** ▶ **Species 1009 – AA** (gaseous life form with no name) ▶ **Species 1011 – HH** (known as future humans)
2 SCIENTISTS EXPLORERS	Humanity can expect an increased level of contact and intervention. Some may have the basic agenda of a quest for knowledge. Intervention to meet an objective is acceptable but typically wouldn't involve a planetary invasion. The species may attempt to manipulate humanity from the background or support our ongoing development.	▶ **Grays up to 1979** ▶ **Draconians at various times in history** ▶ **Species 282 – CC** (known as "Horned Grays") ▶ **Species 213 – CC** (known as "Space Pixies")
3 INVADERS OCCUPIERS SETTLERS	This category sees Earth as a potential home world and could come either in peace or as would-be conquerors. Motivations may include a dying home planet or just empire growth. Alien refugees from an intergalactic war may also fall into this category. This category will have a profound impact on humanity and most scientists agree that any intervention will be hostile.	▶ **Little Green Men** ▶ **Draconians** ▶ ██████████████
4 SCAVENGERS	Earth and its resources, including humanity and the incredible diversity of biomatter, will be of interest to many scavengers. For example, humans may be taken from the planet to become part of a slave labor force. Although an unremarkable planet in terms of minerals and ores, Earth has elements that are considered valuable elsewhere in the universe.	▶ **Grays after 1979** ▶ **Little Green Men in some scenarios** ▶ **Species 441 – DD** (known as "Rigelians")
5 EXTERMINATORS	This is an extremely hostile category. With various motivations, exterminators have a mission to extinguish life on Earth. Maybe they will become new occupiers, but occupation will be preceded by the eradication of all human life. Currently, we only know of one species with this agenda and this is only applicable under specific conditions around the movement of their home world. But there are others out there who see any species different from their own as a nuisance to be destroyed, much as one might think nothing of wiping out a colony of pesky ants.	▶ **Insectoids** (known as "The Species")

Caught a spider looking at me strangely yesterday but he's an arachnid – does that count?

ALIEN KNOWLEDGE 101

ALIENS IN JUDGEMENT

In extraterrestrial defense circles, they call it the Roffey Syndrome, after the Oxford scientist Steve Roffey who first theorized it back in 1978. Having spent time in Tibet and having witnessed a Nordic visitation, Dr Roffey was the first to link the disappearance of alien worlds with the existence of superbeings who may arrive, sit in judgement, then decide the fate of a species.

DR STEVE ROFFEY

"I completed my research in the summer of 1977, noting with some interest that the Perilo system in an outer quadrant had disappeared. I mentioned this to the milkman but he seemed most disinterested. It was not until I was privileged enough to hear the Nordics speaking in Tibet that I realized just how vulnerable we are to their strong moralistic line of questioning. I was able to ask one of the aliens if it knew anything about the disappearance. It looked sheepish and promptly dematerialized."

Roffey went on to suggest that some species may develop to such a degree that they feel they are able to sit in judgement over what they see as lesser species. We have no evidence that the Nordics fit into this category but we have prepared some guidelines as follows.

▶ OUR AMAZING PLANET

If you're approached by any form of superbeing asking you to make a case for humanity's survival, think very carefully before deciding whether you're best qualified to answer the question on behalf of the billions on the planet. If you decide you are, try to relax and take the superbeing through the amazing things about our planet and people. Mention the wonderful biodiversity on Earth; leave out any extinctions and if necessary say they were dead when we got here.

▶ DON'T MENTION THE WARS!

Steer the focus away from any war or conflict. If they ask, just infer that we've had a few "fall-outs" from time to time but on the whole we're a peaceful and curious species.

▶ DON'T UNDERWHELM THEM!

Don't rush to locations such as Stonehenge as there's a danger that a superbeing will be distinctly underwhelmed by our ability to put large stones on top of each other. In terms of other locations to show any aliens who stand in judgement over humanity, try Venice (out of season), Harvard, or any great sporting events. Avoid New York in the summer, war zones, or Oxford Street in London.

▶ ACT SMART!

Don't get drawn into any discussion on time dilation, string theory, or why they cancelled the TV series *Firefly*. One day mankind may understand these things but as yet they're beyond our intelligence. It may be worth learning a few clever quips in binary as that always goes down well.

⚠ IF ALL ELSE FAILS
USE SIMPLE BUT CONFUSING RIDDLES

"WHY DID THE CHICKEN CROSS THE ROAD?"
"TO GET TO THE OTHER SIDE."
Once you've delivered your punch line, pause and raise your eyebrows as if you're trying to confirm that the superbeing has understood. The trick is to hint that there's some deep meaning. In some instances, a superbeing may well see something that we don't.

 MINISTRY OF ALIEN DEFENSE

ALIEN TECHNOLOGY MATRIX

Planners love a matrix and as soon as the Alien Motivation Matrix was completed a technology one was promptly tabled. On a serious note, it's important in any military assessment that both intent and capability are assessed, and the Alien Technology Matrix below was added to the Alien Motivation Matrix in 2009 after a seriously long meeting. After all, there may be millions of hostile alien civilizations out there in the universe but many won't have the technologies to wage war, while others may lack the power-creation expertise to devise an interstellar propulsion system. The table below summarizes our current knowledge about known alien species.

LIFE FORM	SPACE TRAVEL	SOLAR SYSTEM TRAVEL	GALAXY TRAVEL	UNIVERSE TRAVEL	DIMENSIONAL TRAVEL	EXAMPLES FROM KNOWN SPECIES
T0 MICROBIAL LIFE	✓ On solar winds/asteroids	✓	✗	✗	✗	▶ Space fungus ▶ Draconian fungus
T1 PRE-INDUSTRIAL LIFE	✗	✗	✗	✗	✗	▶ Species 611 – AA
T2 CIVILIZATION (NON-SPACE)	✗	✗	✗	✗	✗	▶ Species 678 – HH
T3 TERRAN NORMAL	✓	✗	✗	✗	✗	▶ Current Earth
T4 SOLAR SYSTEM COLONIZERS	✓	✓	✗	✗	✗	▶ Earth plus 100 years ▶ Species 441 – DD ▶ The Skulkrin Imperium
T5 GALACTIC MOVERS	✓	✓	✓	✗	✗	▶ Grays/Little Green Men ▶ Species 282 – CC "Horned Grays" ▶ Species 213 – CC "Space Pixies"
T6 UNIVERSE MOVERS	✓	✓	✓	✓	✗	▶ Draconians ▶ Insectoids
T7 GOD-LIKE ABILITIES	✓	✓	✓	✓	✓	▶ Nordics ▶ Mirror Men ▶ Species 1009 – AA Gaseous lifeform ▶ Species 1011 – HH "future humans"

The lizards are already here! (handwritten note, T6 row)

17

THE GRAYS (ROSWELL GRAYS, ZETANS)

The Grays are perhaps the most recognizable aliens for most of humanity due to their portrayal in movies and fiction and, in particular, the popular *X-Files* series of the 1990s. With this in mind, there are more misconceptions about the Grays than any other species, with significant confusion around both their motivation and their level of contact with the human race. Many alien watchers believe that the Grays are the only extraterrestrials to have visited Earth and see them as a paternal influence, guiding humankind, but as things stand at the moment the truth is far more sinister.

Initially the Grays – the only alien species with whom we have had formal and protracted contact – were regarded primarily as scientists and observers, but the past 50 years have seen a massive shift in our relationship with them and it has now broken down to the point where the Grays should be considered as potential invaders of our planet.

MOST EXPERTS NOW AGREE THAT THE GRAYS' DESPERATION FOR BIODIVERSE MATTER AND THE FACT THAT THEIR SPECIES STANDS ON THE BRINK OF EXTINCTION MEAN THAT HUMANITY WILL FACE A GRAY INVASION WITHIN THE NEXT 10–20 YEARS.

APPEARANCE AND ABILITIES

WHAT WE KNOW!

The species known as the Grays comprises small humanoid life forms with an oversized head compared with human standards. We have little information on the natural lifespan of Gray individuals, but there's some evidence to indicate that a Gray transfers its mental intelligence into a new body once its existing body reaches a certain age.

In most of the human contact with Grays, only subtle differences have been observed between individuals, making it quite a challenge to tell them apart. Grays don't refer to themselves by any individual name.

I've seen bigger!

HEIGHT	3-5 feet (1-1.5 meters)
WEIGHT	44-88 pounds (20-40 kg)
COLOR	Pallid gray color with a damp texture
LIKES	Pasta, sneezing, and cats
DISLIKES	Ping Pong and backwards running

PHYSICAL FEATURES

▶ Bones are thin but very flexible, being made of malleable cartilage. Grays may have adapted their bodies to cope with the demands of space travel.

▶ Eyes are large, black, and slanting upwards, with very thin "eyelids" that rarely seem to close. Gray eyes are particularly sensitive to fine particles such as dust.

▶ Grays have long arms that end in long, slender fingers; each hand has three fingers and a thin thumb. Although not every Gray alien is exactly the same, the ratio between height, arm and leg length is always the same, hinting that each Gray, in fact, is a clone – although the species allows for some diversity.

▶ Lack of any sexual organs. Grays are asexual and have no concept of male and female.

▶ A Gray has a small mouth and tiny airways instead of a nose. Grays can breathe Earth's atmosphere but appear very sensitive to pollution.

ABILITIES

▶ Grays have strong telepathic abilities and rarely emit any noise from their mouths. They have the ability to engage in regular communication through telepathy but also to aggressively plant concepts into their victims' brains and even control their will and movement. They can create a neural network that enables them to share knowledge between themselves.

ALIEN KNOWLEDGE 101
THE GRAY AGENDA

The Grays are primarily interested in both human DNA and the wider biodiversity of our planet. The Grays are master manipulators of DNA and evolution, thousands of years ahead of anything we can conceive, but this hasn't stopped them leading their species into an evolutionary dead end. We have documented evidence that the Grays switched long ago to cloning to reproduce and that this technology worked for them for tens of thousands of years. We also suspect that they've spliced alien DNA into their own at various points in their history. However, they now face a major crisis for reasons even they cannot fathom: their clones are increasingly weak and unable to survive. Hence, for much of the 20th century and onwards, the Grays looked to Earth to satisfy their need for biodiversity. ▬▬▬▬▬▬▬▬▬▬

08/02 hg

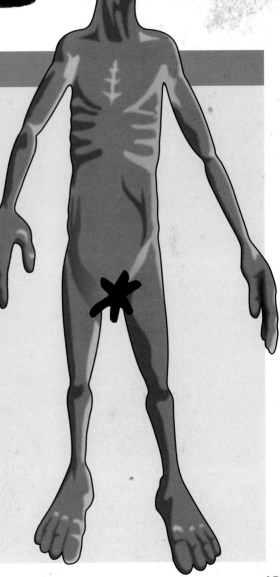

This guy starred in Close Encounters of the Third Kind, The X-Files, and Stargate. He must have a good agent.

ALIEN MOTIVATION MATRIX: 2/4
SCIENTISTS OR SCAVENGERS?

With the breakdown of the Grays' treaty with humanity in 1979, their agenda has shifted to one of resource collection. They are, therefore, now classed as a scavenger species. They are interested in DNA and biomatter of all descriptions and so we must assume they that would be prepared to strip our planet and leave it a sterile, lifeless rock if it ensured that their species could survive.

ALIEN TECHNOLOGY MATRIX: T5
GALACTIC MOVERS

The Grays are experienced space travellers but haven't yet traversed the whole universe. Distance is a factor for this species and it will impact on any Earth-invasion strategy. For example, it'll take time for the Grays to bring in any reinforcements. However, despite all of their technological knowledge, Gray civilization is facing the threat of extinction due to the gradual degradation of their DNA material.

THE GRAYS ARE DESPERATE TO SOLVE THEIR CLONING CRISIS AND SEE THE RICH BIOMASS OF EARTH AS THE BEST CHANCE THEY HAVE OF SAVING THEIR OWN SPECIES. FROM THEIR VIEWPOINT, THEY'VE TRIED TALKING AND IT HASN'T WORKED, SO HUMANITY MUST BE PREPARED FOR A MAJOR GRAY INVASION IN THE NEAR FUTURE.

ALIEN KNOWLEDGE 101

⚙ TECHNOLOGY

Known as a Type 1 Gray Saucer, this type of ship has been spotted over Earth countless times. Finally, one crashed in Roswell, New Mexico in 1947 and has been reverse-engineered for over 50 years.

1. Silver non-reflective metal (unknown).
2. Metal dome housing the Command Bridge.
3. Shield nodes around the vessel, generating a powerful protective shield (energy type unknown).
4. Energy pulse weapons (can be used in atmosphere or space).
5. Rotating band believed to be linked to the ship's gravitational propulsion system.
6. A wide strip of moving metallic liquid that pulsates when the ship is in flight – known as "the glowing band."
7. Tractor beam – used for abductions and capable of lifting many hundreds of tons.
8. Retractable landing stairs.
9. Landing struts.
10. Sealed hyper-drive unit.
11. Propulsion unit (anti-gravity).
12. Liquid display linked to ship's systems.
13. Bio-computers, with bioengineered "processing units."
14. Biomass that feeds into the ship.
15. Operation table.
16. Experimentation chamber – the location is familiar to millions of abduction victims around the world.
17. Cryogenic chambers for samples.
18. Tractor beam hatchway.
19. Sealed pods, purpose unknown.
20. Escape saucer – there's one of these mini-saucers in Area 51 but it hasn't been possible to activate it.
21. Sleep booths that double as cryogenic pods for crew members.
22. Command bridge.
23. Biological computer and controls.
24. Five flight seats.
25. Flight control method is unclear; theorized to be a neural link.

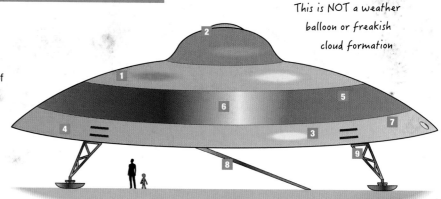

This is NOT a weather balloon or freakish cloud formation

MAIN DECK

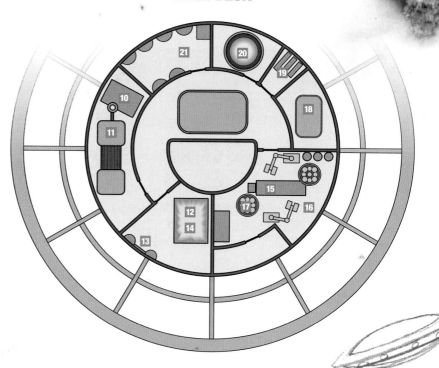

COMMAND BRIDGE

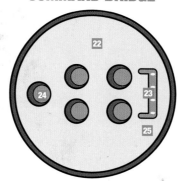

> **DESPITE HAVING ACCESS TO A CRASHED TYPE 1, TO HUNDREDS OF DEBRIS PARTS AND HAVING THE EXPERIENCE OF SENDING HUMANS ON BOARD GRAY VESSELS DURING THE TIME OF THE GREADA TREATY, WE ARE STILL A LONG WAY FROM UNDERSTANDING THE PHYSICS AND DYNAMICS OF THESE SHIPS.**
> **UNNAMED SOURCE 244, AREA 51**

 SOCIETY *Say "no" to alien abductions!*

The Grays have an egalitarian social structure, with no apparent ranks and little hierarchy. Even though humanity has spent far more time with this species than any other, we're still unsure as to their level of telepathic communication. For example, we know that they can read human minds and implant ideas or suggestions but we know little about the extent of the neural network that the Grays have established to link themselves together. Our current working hypothesis is that the Grays have some kind of implant that enables them to establish this mind link and that it has become their main path of communication.

With this in mind, we suspect the Grays' home world to be a very boring place. Everyone knows pretty much everything. Pop quizzes are a waste of time and card games pointless. The Grays come across as emotionless aliens and we expect this to be reflected in a society that's very sterile, ordered, and balanced.

ORIGIN AND HOME WORLD

There's a fundamental disagreement on this subject. According to the Grays, their home system is Zeta Reticuli, a wide binary star system in the southern constellation of Reticulum. However, the Draconians insist that they genetically designed the Grays as a slave species eons ago and implanted this history. Grays regard this allegation as an illogical insult.

The Grays' quest for biomatter has taken them across millions of galaxies as they search for the right DNA sequences they could use to repair their own failing strings. We know that they've experimented with hybridization, trying to introduce new biomatter into their lineage by selective breeding.

TYPE 2 SAUCERS

Since 1980, UFO watchers have reported the sighting of new, slightly larger saucers over Earth. Type 1 saucers are 131-164 feet (40-50 meters) across, whereas the new ships, known as Type 2s, are believed to measure well over 328 feet (100 meters) in diameter.

▶ FACT OR FICTION?

The Grays have been featured in more movies than any other species but often these portrayals have caused confusion among alien watchers across the globe. Here's a quick run-down of some of the most famous blurred lines between fact and fiction.

There was a government program in *The X-Files* that allowed the Grays to abduct people.

FACT The Grays did in fact have a formal treaty with the American government until 1979 and under this treaty they were free to take a certain number of people providing they were returned.

The Grays are visitors who want to get to know us, like in *Close Encounters of the Third Kind*.

FICTION The Grays know humanity well enough and they've run out of time and patience with us. They've been aggressively abducting people for decades and now stand at the brink of a major invasion of the planet.

Grays look so sweet and helpless. They're actually rather cute, as in the movie *Paul*.

FICTION We wish this were the case. The movie *Paul* was hilarious but, in reality, the Grays have a far more sinister agenda. *Paul* was reasonably accurate in its physical portrayal of Grays, apart from the fact that they cannot dematerialize at will.

In the movie *Signs*, the Grays seem obsessed with making crop circles.

FICTION The Grays have never made crop circles. The only marks they leave behind are the burn marks from their saucer landings.

Is it true that there are Gray saucers hidden away in Area 51?

FACT There are many crashed alien ships around the world, including Gray saucers, but this doesn't mean that we understand all of the technology within such ships. Scientists have spent decades reverse-engineering these ships and we're just about getting to grips with some of the basics.

LITTLE GREEN MEN (LGM, MARTIANS)

After the Grays, Little Green Men (LGM) are probably the most recognizable alien species to the general populace. They were caricatured in countless pulp science fiction novels during the 1930s and 1940s and have frequently been referred to as Martians.

Little Green Men are an unpredictable and envious species of alien and this, combined with their passion for ray guns, makes them a particularly dangerous opponent for Earth. Their menacing, black, triangle-shaped ships have been seen countless times and files released after the fall of communism in East Germany prove conclusively that Little Green Men were working with the Nazi regime on their early jet fighters. Spiteful, vindictive, and prone to vaporizing things that irritate them, these aren't the sort of aliens with whom you'd want to be trapped in a lift.

THE LITTLE GREEN MEN ARE AN AMBITIOUS SPECIES, LOOKING TO EXPAND THEIR INFLUENCE ACROSS THE GALAXY. THEY MAY HAVE WHAT PSYCHOLOGISTS REFER TO AS AN "INFERIORITY COMPLEX," AS THEY SHY AWAY FROM CONFLICT WITH THOSE THEY CONSIDER TO BE MORE TECHNOLOGICALLY ADVANCED, PREFERRING TO "BULLY" SPECIES TO WHOM THEY FEEL SUPERIOR.

APPEARANCE AND ABILITIES

WHAT WE KNOW!

The species known as Little Green Men are diminutive humanoid life forms with a green hue to their skin. Little Green Men have typically been referred to as "Martians" throughout history.

It's unlikely that Little Green Men would sit idly by as humanity develops deep-space travel and even faster-than-light capability. For this reason they're likely to become particularly dangerous to the planet during the 21st century.

HEIGHT	1 metre
WEIGHT	10–20kg
COLOR	Mottled green in color
LIKES	Ray guns, and acting tough
DISLIKES	Being call a Martian, and the movie *Mars Attacks*

PHYSICAL FEATURES

▶ The species has been seen wearing space suits and sometimes a light form of chain-mail armor.
▶ Physically weak in comparison to humans, they're known to carry small ray guns, which can be lethal.
▶ They're full of bravado when armed and in company with their fellow aliens, but if found alone or injured at a crash site they adopt an almost child-like persona.
▶ Skin is a mottled green color and said to be cool and textured to the touch. They sweat profusely when enraged – which is often – and the tops of their bald green heads are said to pulsate as they fume.
▶ Eyes are bulbous, with a white background and black pupils. Frequently the eyes appear bloodshot and probably have significant blood vessels around them.

ABILITIES

▶ They have some telepathic abilities but can also communicate verbally in what, to humans, sounds like a constant and piercing stream of high-pitched banter. Witnesses have reported hearing words that sound like "yak" and "tak," and it seems that their language is made up entirely of variations on this theme.
▶ Part of the repertoire of the Little Green Men's speech lies in its rhythm and pitch. Orders are given at louder volume, while speeding up and higher pitch indicate irritation; a squealing "laughter" sound has even been noted.

 ## ALIEN KNOWLEDGE 101
THE LITTLE GREEN MEN AGENDA

Classic alien invaders – they're in it for the power

Intelligence suggests that the Little Green Men see humans as lumbering, slow, dim-witted mammals with a low level of intelligence. They have an obvious superiority complex over Earthlings and consider their mastery of interstellar travel to be an example of this. <u>It can be assumed that they wish to maintain this advantage over humanity and some experts suspect their little green hands in various acts of sabotage, particularly on our space projects.</u> For example, in 2012, a reliable source reported that just before NASA lost contact with the Mars Rover probe, blurred pictures were beamed back of what looked like small green humanoids dashing towards it. These images were never released publicly because it was feared this could lead to panic on Earth. Some secretly believed that the Little Green Men <u>sabotaged the vehicle,</u> perhaps to hide their military preparations or the pyramids they built on Mars many years ago.

23/06 9p

 ## ALIEN MOTIVATION MATRIX: 3
INVADERS/OCCUPIERS/SETTLERS

The Little Green Men are classic empire builders. They've enslaved hundreds of worlds throughout their galaxy and are keen to expand their growing power base. They're primarily invaders who take over by conflict, then enslave the local population, often presenting themselves as god-like rulers. If the planet proves to be of little value, they can easily strip it clean then move on.

 ## ALIEN TECHNOLOGY MATRIX: T5
GALACTIC MOVERS

The Little Green Men do have access to very advanced space technology such as the sealed anti-matter drives that power their triangular black ships, but it's thought that they haven't actually created much original technology. They're expert looters and avoid conflict with more advanced species such as the Draconians. The Little Green Men have invaded many worlds and have developed a range of specialized weapons, such as giant tripods, to support their domination of technologically inferior species.

Get your facts right Ministry – these aliens wear armor

GRAY INTELLIGENCE SUGGESTS THAT THEY FREQUENTLY ARRIVE AS MILITARY CONQUERORS, PREFERRING TO USE LOCAL ELITES TO DIVIDE AND RULE THE PLANET. IN SOME CASES, THEY INSTALL THEMSELVES AS RATHER SMALL GODS.

⚙ TECHNOLOGY

A black triangle ship isn't detectable by radar and has the ability to change direction and speed in an instant. It's one of the most frequently spotted alien ships over Earth, most typically found around military installations and air bases.

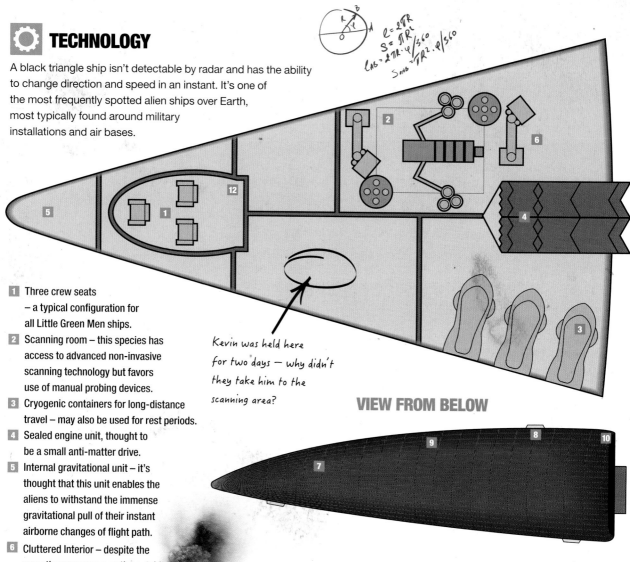

VIEW FROM BELOW

1. Three crew seats – a typical configuration for all Little Green Men ships.

2. Scanning room – this species has access to advanced non-invasive scanning technology but favors use of manual probing devices.

3. Cryogenic containers for long-distance travel – may also be used for rest periods.

4. Sealed engine unit, thought to be a small anti-matter drive.

5. Internal gravitational unit – it's thought that this unit enables the aliens to withstand the immense gravitational pull of their instant airborne changes of flight path.

6. Cluttered Interior – despite the smooth appearance on the outside, the interior of a black triangle ship is cluttered, with pieces of equipment and technology wired in and clearly mismatched; black sticky tape is widely used to secure cables.

7. Covered in black stealth tiles – this technology has been successfully used by the Americans on their stealth program and it's believed that the tiles are primarily designed to make the ship "invisible" in space.

8. Three external light sources.

9. Outside thrusters enable this vessel to move in any direction.

10. Laser nodes on each corner of the ship enable it to fire high-energy beams in any direction. Typically these are set to fire in pulsating bursts.

11. An electric kettle – both crashed ships were found to have electric kettles from Earth. If the Little Green Men see technology they like, they have no problems just blending it with their own. In this case, something about the primitive heating element of an electric kettle attracted them.

THE POWER OF THREE

Typically black triangle ships fly in groups of three and in a tight holding pattern. This has confused some witnesses who believed that they were seeing one ship when in fact there were three of them.

SOCIETY

Little Green Men are known to be ambitious, devious, and sometimes irrational. They're curious by nature but have no interest in interspecies communication unless it directly benefits them. They can appear child-like, selfish, and even mischievous, delighting in matching any human achievements such as high-speed flight and interfering with any human space program.

We know little of how Little Green Men society works. Evidence of their behavior on Earth hints that they have a strict hierarchical structure but one that doesn't prevent an almost constant state of argument, debate, and heated discussion. The aliens appear to have a warrior class and it is believed that these are the only Little Green Men that humans have ever encountered.

Little Green Men are scavengers of other technology and seem to have no concept of "theft" when taking individuals or technology from other worlds. They study humanity purely from the viewpoint of what they can get out of it. Little Green Men are fond of weapons and individuals are rarely seen without their almost stereotypical "ray gun."

ORIGIN AND HOME WORLD

While the Little Green Men have been known to operate from a base on Mars, there has always been some confusion as to the origin of this species. In fact, they originate from near a pulsar known as PSR B1919+21 (or CP1919 as it was previously called) in the constellation of Vulpecula. This system is over 2,200 light years away and as such LGM ships require vast sources of energy to cover such distances.

The species has used its base on Mars to monitor Earth and several other planets of interest in nearby systems. In fact, it's thought that the recent attention of the Grays was one of the factors in the Little Green Men deciding to reopen their Mars site.

> THREE IS A NUMBER OF PARTICULAR RELEVANCE TO LITTLE GREEN MEN, ALTHOUGH WE DON'T KNOW WHY. ALL OF THE SHIPS HAVE SOME FORM OF TRIANGULAR SHAPE. MANY HAVE THREE PROMINENT LIGHTS. THE CREW OF THEIR SMALLER VESSELS IS THREE AND THE SHIPS OFTEN FLY IN A "V-FORMATION" OF THREE SHIPS. ONE THEORY LINKS THIS TO THEIR UNUSUAL PHYSIOLOGY, WHICH PROVIDES MANY OF THEIR INTERNAL ORGANS IN TRIPLICATE.

UNNAMED SOURCE 247, AREA 51

► LITTLE GREEN MEN FACTS

WHY LITTLE GREEN MEN?

The term "Little Green Men" was first coined over 100 years ago on Earth and is considered to be highly offensive to the species. The Little Green Men have watched a lot of Earth television as they study our civilization, their favorite shows including the various Star Trek series and the *Star Wars* movies. In their own language, which has a fiendishly complicated syntax, they refer to themselves as "The Original and Great Master Species of the Galaxy who are Greatly Blessed by the Mighty Ones and who are Brave and have the Power of Three" – that's a rough translation. That's what Little Green Men call themselves; no one else calls them that.

A RARE SPECIES

It's estimated that there are fewer than a billion Little Green Men in the universe, making them one of the rarest alien species we know of. It's thought that their constant infighting almost reduced their civilization to rubble so they decided to start picking on weaker alien species instead.

NEITHER MALE NOR FEMALE

Autopsies on Little Green Men bodies from crash sites on Earth reveal that, in fact, they're neither male nor female, so their description is misleading. A grainy picture of a bloated body was shown to a Nordic contact in Tibet in 2003 as it was suspected that the Little Green Man concerned was of a bigger variety and possibly even a male. Instead, the Nordic just shrugged and hinted that this was simply a fat specimen of no sex.

THE GRAYS LEAD THE WAY

Little Green Men avoid contact with other more advanced alien species. A phenomenon that has confused UFO hunters occurs when an abduction by Grays – with their distinct saucer ships – is followed soon after by an incident with a triangular Little Green Men ship. Experts suggest that the Little Green Men are fearful that the Grays are gaining some advantage through their human experimentation and frequently make follow-up visits to monitor anything of interest.

DRACONIANS (THE FIRST ONES, REPTILIANS)

If every alien invasion scenario was one involving flying saucers, ray guns, and tripods, then we would certainly be clearer about the threat we face. We could spend all of our time and resources on the military defense of our planet. However, the universe is far more complicated than that and there are many species that see <u>stealth and deception</u> as better ways to take control of both the human population and the planet. Of all the covert enemies of this planet, the lizard-like Draconians are the most persistent and dangerous.

Any search on the internet will yields thousands of websites dedicated to what's often termed the "lizard menace." Many are wildly inaccurate, making all kinds of claims about these elusive aliens. Others just sound crazed and delusional, with accusations that all politicians on Earth, and even entire populations, have been replaced by Draconian shape-shifters or clones.

THE DRACONIANS ARE MASTERS OF MISINFORMATION AND WE NOW BELIEVE THAT THE ALIENS THEMSELVES WORK TO FUEL THESE RUMORS AND ACTIVELY SUPPORT THE "LUNATIC FRINGE" ON THE INTERNET. THE DRACONIANS ARE EXPERTS AT HIDING IN PLAIN SIGHT AND WILL DO ANYTHING TO KEEP THEIR MASTER PLAN UNDER WRAPS.

▶ APPEARANCE AND ABILITIES

WHAT WE KNOW! *You know nothing!*

The species known as the Draconians refer to themselves as "The First Ones" and are large, bipedal lizard-like creatures with prominent head ridges. To humans, their most startling aspect is the capability to change form or "shape-shift." This enables Draconians to mimic other species, which makes them particularly dangerous opponents. It's believed that other reptilian species have similar capabilities.

Draconians have perfected techniques in the power of suggestion and can exercise significant control over human minds.

Humans - you are a puny species!

HEIGHT	6.5-8 feet (2-2.5 meters)
WEIGHT	198-287 pounds (90-130kg)
COLOR	Brown, smooth and scaly in places
LIKES	Byzantine politics and reptile charities
DISLIKES	Open confrontation, smoking, mammals

PHYSICAL FEATURES

▶ Skin is scaly in places but is reported to be cool and smooth in other areas. It may be that a warrior class has developed armored scales, with overlapping plates of hardened shell.

▶ Eyes are yellow with vertical black slits for pupils. They're said to move rapidly and can roll independently of each other – which humans find very unsettling.

▶ Draconians are able to breathe on Earth but are sensitive to many sprays such as perfumes and even smoke.

▶ They don't have ears in a human sense but "hear" through vibrations. They're very sensitive in this respect and will often tilt their heads as they pick up movements far away.

▶ Draconian hands extend to two or three large fingers with claws at the end. The claws can grow up to 4 inches (10cm) but this length is considered "uncouth" by the Draconians and many creatures file their claws.

ABILITIES

▶ Draconians are typically very powerful creatures. When angry, they can spit bile-like acid that will burn human skin.

▶ Most important of all, Draconians have the ability to "shape-shift" into different forms. In the 1950s it was believed that some form of chemical release "fooled" people into believing Draconians changed form, but then TV cameras captured some actual occurences and proved the phenomenon beyond doubt. Science is at a loss to explain the shape-shifting abilities of Draconians.

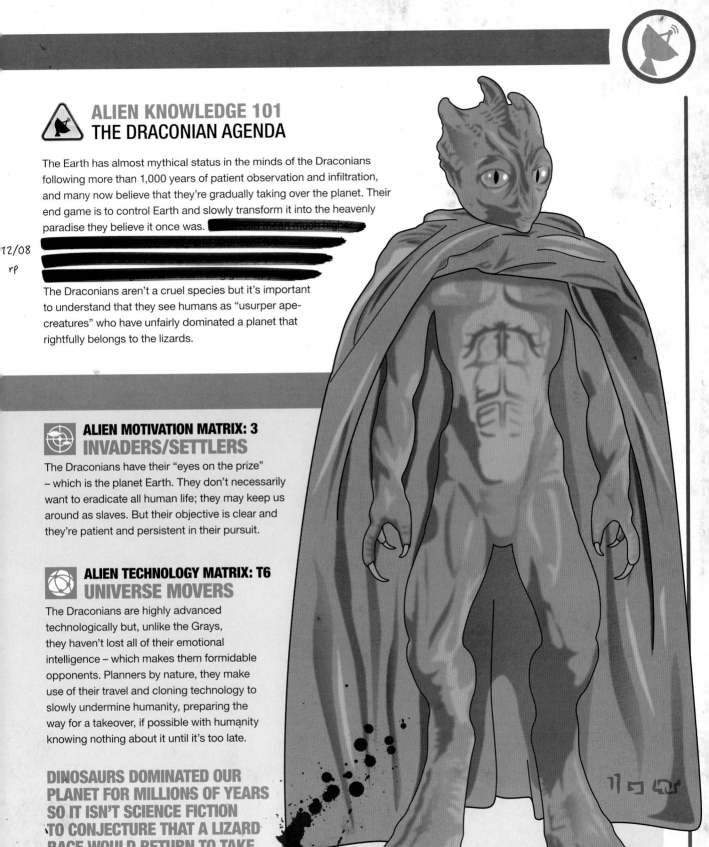

ALIEN KNOWLEDGE 101
THE DRACONIAN AGENDA

The Earth has almost mythical status in the minds of the Draconians following more than 1,000 years of patient observation and infiltration, and many now believe that they're gradually taking over the planet. Their end game is to control Earth and slowly transform it into the heavenly paradise they believe it once was. ██████████████████████

12/08

rp

The Draconians aren't a cruel species but it's important to understand that they see humans as "usurper ape-creatures" who have unfairly dominated a planet that rightfully belongs to the lizards.

ALIEN MOTIVATION MATRIX: 3
INVADERS/SETTLERS

The Draconians have their "eyes on the prize" – which is the planet Earth. They don't necessarily want to eradicate all human life; they may keep us around as slaves. But their objective is clear and they're patient and persistent in their pursuit.

ALIEN TECHNOLOGY MATRIX: T6
UNIVERSE MOVERS

The Draconians are highly advanced technologically but, unlike the Grays, they haven't lost all of their emotional intelligence – which makes them formidable opponents. Planners by nature, they make use of their travel and cloning technology to slowly undermine humanity, preparing the way for a takeover, if possible with humanity knowing nothing about it until it's too late.

DINOSAURS DOMINATED OUR PLANET FOR MILLIONS OF YEARS SO IT ISN'T SCIENCE FICTION TO CONJECTURE THAT A LIZARD RACE WOULD RETURN TO TAKE THE EARTH AS ITS OWN.

ALIEN KNOWLEDGE 101

⚙️ TECHNOLOGY

The Draconian "pod ship" is designed for stealth and to conceal itself on alien worlds. In the absence of a more secure base, it provides numerous "pods" via which Draconians can clone alien life forms and infiltrate their societies.

Pod ships have only rarely been caught on camera and are equipped with powerful stealth technology that seems to create the illusion of being able to see through a vessel.

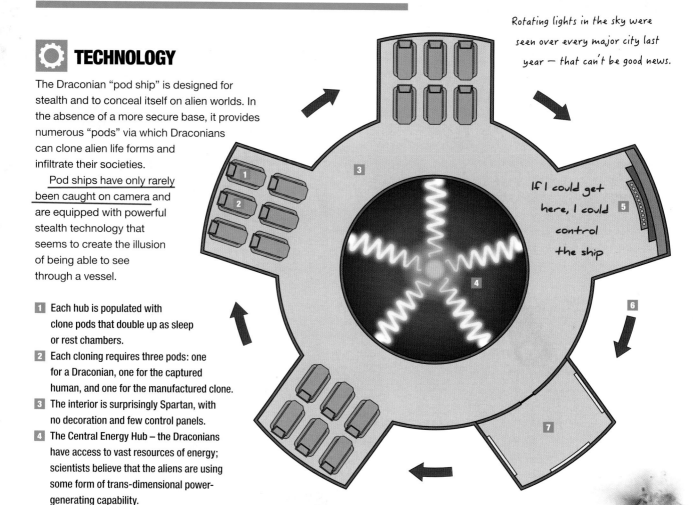

Rotating lights in the sky were seen over every major city last year — that can't be good news.

If I could get here, I could control the ship

1. Each hub is populated with clone pods that double up as sleep or rest chambers.
2. Each cloning requires three pods: one for a Draconian, one for the captured human, and one for the manufactured clone.
3. The interior is surprisingly Spartan, with no decoration and few control panels.
4. The Central Energy Hub – the Draconians have access to vast resources of energy; scientists believe that the aliens are using some form of trans-dimensional power-generating capability.
5. Navigation hub.
6. Ship spins rapidly in flight.
7. Abduction Room – the function of this room is uncertain, although some sources suggest that it's used for abductions and implants.
8. Reflective tiles give an illusion of invisibility.
9. When landed, the ship generates a powered stealth field.
10. Pod ships are designed to spend long periods of time "cloaked" – almost invisible.
11. Pod cruisers are said to be between 164 and 328 feet (50 and 100 meters) in diameter.
12. The landing struts on a pod ship contain long root-like metal tendrils that reach down into a planet; it's believed that these are used to extract water or perhaps geothermal energy.

> **DRACONIANS MAKE USE OF NANO-TECHNOLOGY TO MONITOR HUMANITY, DEPLOYING THE MOST ADVANCED IMPLANT TECHNOLOGY EVER SEEN. THEY HAVE BEEN SEEN USING SMALL WRIST DEVICES FOR VARIOUS ACTIVITIES SUCH AS LOCATION TRACKING.**
> **TECHNOLOGY ADVISER, UK CABINET BRIEFING, 2013**

THE CLOAKED SHIP

You can sometimes catch a glimpse of a cloaked vessel as it will occasionally shimmer, particularly in smoky conditions.

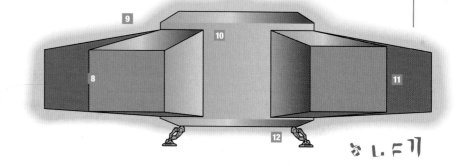

SOCIETY

Draconians are highly political creatures, living in very structured, ordered societies in which a slight mispronunciation can result in deep offense and shunning. Their approach to all things is typically indirect. They'll avoid direct confrontation where possible, preferring the Byzantine approaches of infiltration, conspiracy, and control by proxy. For example, as hatchlings they're encouraged to engage in fiendishly complex and cruel mind games with the rest of their brood, with the most influential "child" becoming the favored one.

They greatly value power over just wealth and firmly believe that humans are a second-class species. Something Draconians often point out is how humans kill each other. In Draconian society, killing another lizard is strictly taboo. However, they think nothing of eating their young if the hatchlings don't come up to standard, so they shouldn't be too judgemental just because some humans like a bit of "rough and tumble."

What are they trying to hide?

🪐 ORIGIN AND HOME WORLD

The Draconians have visited Earth for millennia and are now believed to have made their home in the Draco constellation, on a rocky planet around the bright star Gamma Draconis or Etamin. This is around 148 light years from Earth. However, Draconian myth-legend is that Earth is one of their original homes and that a species of humanoid reptiles still lives deep within the planet.

The Draconians are an ancient race in the universe and certainly regard themselves as superior to many of the alien species they encounter. We know that they fought a great war against the Insectoids that spanned many galaxies. We're unaware of the current status of the Draconians and the Insectoids but they certainly won't be sending each other Christmas cards.

> **LITTLE IS KNOWN OF THEIR ACTUAL HOME WORLD. GRAY INTELLIGENCE SUGGESTS THAT IT'S A DRY, BARREN, VOLCANIC WORLD, COVERED IN VAST STONE TEMPLES AND UNIVERSITIES, SOME OF WHICH ARE THOUSANDS OF YEARS OLD. IT'S SAID THAT THE DRACONIAN LIBRARIES CONTAIN NEARLY EVERY BOOK EVER PUBLISHED IN THE UNIVERSE, INCLUDING THE LOST WORKS OF HOMER, THE COMEDIES OF ARISTOTLE, AND ALL JACKIE COLLINS'S BOOKS.**

MEN IN BLACK REPORT – AGENT MIB788 – LAGOS, NIGERIA

▶ A NOTE ON CONSPIRACIES

DRACONIAN CONSPIRACIES

The Draconians are experts at creating conspiracy theories and it has been estimated that over 53% of the alien sites on the internet are either directly run or funded by the Draconians to help spread confusion. This species delights in creating misinformation and chaos among humans and has been linked to everything from mock Gray abductions to kidnapping and cloning world leaders. They've also been closely tied to the New Age movement, seeing it as a chance to pacify humanity by stealth.

ISN'T EVERY FAMOUS PERSON A CLONE?

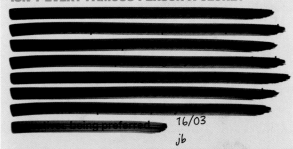

16/03
jb

THE MOON LANDING HAPPENED, RIGHT?

Almost 50% of the population now doubt that the moon landings of 1969 ever took place, but this is one conspiracy the Ministry of Alien Defense can clear up. On July 20, 1969, the Apollo 11 lunar module landed on Earth's moon. That's a fact. Were the aliens pleased about it? No way. In fact the Little Green Men were livid, believing that they'd already claimed the Moon for themselves. However, they did little more than lodge a formal complaint with the relevant authority before concentrating on their plans to take over the planet.

NEW LEVELS OF SNEAKINESS

Through the limited intelligence we have on the secretive Draconians, we know that they've been involved in virtually every field of espionage and deception on the planet. Their most recent areas of activity have included cyber-crime and in 2010 they were thought to have masterminded a major security breach of the US military's mainframe in which they slightly amended millions of fields of data, doing an estimated $500 million worth of damage.

INSECTOIDS (THE HIVE, THE SPECIES)

Of all the species currently known to us, the Insectoids are perhaps the most "alien" to humanity. We have no direct experience of these creatures and all the information we have has come to us via the Grays or captured Draconian clones. In fact we don't even know how the species refers to itself; the Grays refer to them simply as the "Hive."

The Insectoids are a highly xenophobic species who consider all other life forms to be akin to pollution. They migrate from one system or galaxy to another, with their home nests being made on great hollowed-out asteroids and planetoids. It isn't yet understood what motivates a migration of the colony but our best deduction is that the purpose is resource utilization. In other words, the Insectoid hive moves into a system, strips it bare, and then moves on to the next, eradicating any life forms within hundreds of light years.

ACCORDING TO THE GRAYS, THE INSECTOIDS WILL NOT TOLERATE ANY ALIEN SPECIES WITHIN A SPECIFIC RANGE OF THEIR HOME WORLD OR NEST – WHICH IS WHERE THEIR RULING "QUEEN" IS BASED. THEY AREN'T INTERESTED IN LEARNING ABOUT OTHER LIFE FORMS, EMPIRE BUILDING OR ALLIANCES – FOR THEM, ALL LIFE IS SEEN AS EXPENDABLE.

▶ APPEARANCE AND ABILITIES

WHAT WE KNOW!

Through eons of evolution, the Insectoids have developed what's known as a "command bug" to coordinate their growing empire. Their Queen used to serve this purpose, but now these intelligent creatures can create and adapt orders "on site" and according to the conditions.

An Insectoid is bipedal with a sizeable brain and its slim body is lightly armored with bone. It can communicate either by emitting clicks or by releasing chemical elements. All soldier drones are equipped with tougher bone armor with a slimy coating that makes key areas of their bodies – such as the thorax – highly resistant to energy weapons.

HEIGHT	Unknown
WEIGHT	Unknown
COLOR	Unknown
LIKES	Other Insectoids, their Queen, and 1980s synth pop
DISLIKES	All other life forms, non-binary languages

PHYSICAL FEATURES

▶ It's unlikely that you'll encounter an Insectoid in any battle for Earth. The common element is their insect-like appearance such as a body or thorax and mandibles.

▶ Although referred to as the Insectoids, several of the variations currently known to us have a distinctly arachnid feel to them.

▶ All types of Insectoids have the same core elements, which include antennae (their primary communication and sensory organ), thorax (core of the body), compound eyes, and mandibles (ranging from delicate scientific tweezers to those capable of cutting through steel).

Practice on the ants outside

ABILITIES

▶ We have no definite information on the speed and agility of Insectoids but alien biologists on Earth predict that their capabilities broadly match those of insects on Earth, so we can expect running speeds of up to 50mph (80km/hr).

▶ Importantly, no Insectoid variation feels any pain or emotion. The higher classes operate on detached logic, their decision-making unbiased by any emotional or compassionate response. Lower down the scale, worker drones will willingly sacrifice themselves to support the colony.

▶ The Insectoid species has the ability to create billions of additional life forms as required. Over millions of years they have perfected their reproductive process, which now takes place in humid tunnel-like caves and artificial caverns.

ALIEN KNOWLEDGE 101
THE INSECTOID AGENDA

This is one area we're very clear on – if an Insectoid ship moves into our solar system we can be sure that the plan will be to eradicate all life on Earth. By the time one of their larger hive ships enters, we can be 100% sure that humanity faces a battle for its very survival.

The Insectoids travel around different galaxies in an apparently random pattern, sometimes moving thousands of light years from their current home. They maintain some presence in their system of origin but don't seem to have a "home world" in the sense that we understand. Rather, their home is wherever the Queen in based.

Remember to buy an extra-large can of bug spray

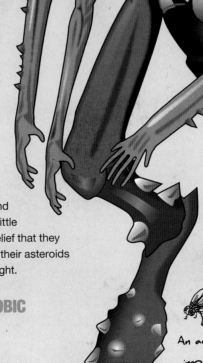

◀ **COMMAND BUG**

This is an artist's impression of an Insectoid command bug based on information supplied by the Grays during their interaction with humanity.

ALIEN MOTIVATION MATRIX: 5

EXTERMINATORS

The Insectoids aren't empire builders in the traditional sense but their presence in a system requires that all other life forms be eradicated. It's believed that they then go on to use all of the resources in the location before the hive continues on its intergalactic migrations across the universe.

ALIEN TECHNOLOGY MATRIX: T6

UNIVERSE MOVERS

With the power-generation and propulsion technology to send ships across the universe, the Insectoids have developed far beyond humanity and even other advanced species such as the Grays. Little is known of Insectoid technology other than our belief that they possess a caste of brain creatures that can power their asteroids and planetoid hive ships far beyond the speed of light.

THE INSECTOID SPECIES IS XENOPHOBIC TO SUCH A DEGREE THAT ANY ALIEN INFLUENCE MUST BE ERADICATED. IT MAY BE THAT IN THE PAST THEIR CULTURE WAS MORE BALANCED AND OPEN, BUT NOW HUMANITY IS FACED WITH A TRULY FRIGHTENING OPPONENT.

An artist's impression of a common bug!

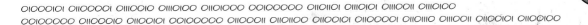

OIOOOIOI OIIOOOOI OIIIOOIO OIIIOIOO OIIOIOOO OOIOOOOO OIIOIIOI OIIIOIOI OIIIOOII OIIOIOO
OOIOOOOO OIIOOIIO OIIOOIOI OOIOOOOO OIIOOOII OIIIOIIOO OIIOIOOI OIIOOOOI OIIOIIO OIIOOII OIIOIOI OIIOOIOO

31

ALIEN KNOWLEDGE 101

SOCIETY

Any comparison with insect life forms on Earth is useful to a degree: for example, Insectoids still inhabit "nests" and are centrally governed by a Queen. They've also evolved specialized creatures such as soldiers and workers, as with ant colonies on Earth. However, it must be remembered that their hive is thousands of years ahead in terms of evolution.

The Insectoids have had powered space flight for eons and their T6 listing on the Alien Technology Matrix means that they're capable of travelling across the known universe and generating the massive amounts of energy required. It's important, therefore, not to assume that their ant-like social structure is a low-technology civilization. The level of specialism in the hive has seen the development not only of soldiers and workers but also a builder drone, command bug, and a large jelly-type mass known by the Grays as a mind bug.

ORIGIN AND HOME WORLD

The Insectoids are believed to have originated in the NGC 7378 galaxy in the Aquarius constellation. It's thought that their species is one of the oldest life forms in the universe and that its adaptability has made it one of the most successful. The planet T-78388-7378 is identified as the home world of the Insectoids by the Grays but even they have never visited this quadrant of space.

Insects became the dominant species on T-78388-7378 and over several million years developed the social structure, language, and technology to expand into their immediate space. According to legend, the Insectoids were originally a peaceful species, content to ignore aliens unless they directly threatened the hive. However, it's believed that a devastating early war with a now long-forgotten alien species warped the governing psychology of the Insectoids such that they cannot now tolerate any alien life form. The planet T-78388-7378 itself is believed to have been sterilized of any life.

THE INSECTOIDS ARE EXPERTS IN GENETIC MANIPULATION AND CAN QUICKLY ADAPT THEIR CORE MODELS, PARTICULARLY THE SOLDIERS, TO MEET THE CHALLENGE OF A PARTICULAR OPPONENT OR ENVIRONMENT. THIS IS THE REAL STRENGTH OF THE HIVE. AN OPPONENT MIGHT DESTROY BILLIONS OF SOLDIERS USING A NEW WEAPON BUT THE INSECTOIDS WILL SIMPLY DEVELOP A VARIANT THAT CAN COMBAT THE WEAPON OR IS RESISTANT TO IT.

▶ INSECTOID TYPES

The Insectoid species has taken specialism to an extreme – developing hundreds of different castes to undertake the myriad tasks involved in sustaining a hive of billions of creatures. This section outlines the key types currently known and most likely to be encountered during any invasion of Earth. There are doubtless others that are unknown outside Insectoid space. Both the Grays and the Draconians maintain an immense buffer zone between their space and that of the Insectoids.

> **"INSECTS ARE THE GREAT SUCCESS STORY OF LIFE ON EARTH IN EVERY MEASURE SO IT'S NOT A SURPRISE THAT THEY HAVE EVOLVED AS THE PRIME SPECIES ON OTHER WORLDS.**
> **DR SOO JAN-LEE, EXTRATERRESTRIAL ENTOMOLOGIST**

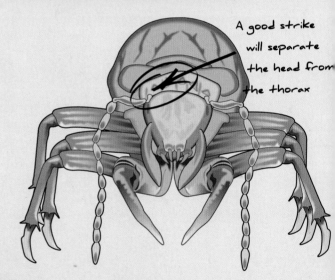

A good strike will separate the head from the thorax

▲ WORKER DRONES
CLASSICS, HIVE BUGS

Colorless and transparent, worker drones are designed for general labor, tunnelling, and carrying. They're blind and move by using their two long antennae. These creatures are basically defenseless: although they can bite with their mandibles, drones lack the intelligence to do anything other than follow orders. It's estimated that around 70% of an Insectoid colony is made up of worker drones. They're expendable and work in vast swarms.

▶ SOLDIER DRONES
FIGHTERS, WARRIOR BUGS

These terrifying armored Insectoids
are the mainstay of the attack swarm.
Armed with various configurations of
stings, jaws, and pointed legs, these
creatures are fearless killers that will
attempt to destroy any opponent
regardless of the cost to themselves.
Most operate on six legs and can be
adapted to carry weapons such as
poison bombs or acid sprays.

How does it fire these jets of acid?

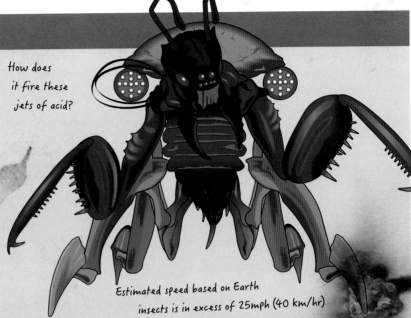

Estimated speed based on Earth insects is in excess of 25mph (40 km/hr)

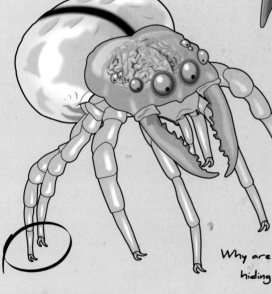

◀ SCIENCE BUGS
INVENTORS, 2.0 BUGS

The armor-less science bug is only found inside the main
hive or an asteroid ship. They have eight eyes and a
detachable brain stem that enables them to be relocated
on to a different body if required. This has enabled these
specialist workers to develop their science and engineering
skills. They have a set of delicate mandibles specially
designed for detailed work. The body is translucent, with
a clear black string running through the center of it.

Why are they hiding this?

▶ MIND BUGS
MIND SLUGS, KINGS

Not even the Grays have seen an Insectoid mind
bug. It's believed that these vast, sprawling creatures
exist only inside asteroid ships and are fed by slave
drones. These Insectoids are said to be the collective
intelligence of the Insectoid species, operating
almost as computer servers, storing knowledge and
experience on individual creatures. It's thought that
each Insectoid hive ship has only one such bug and
therefore it would be an obvious target for any attack.

CLASSIFIED INFORMATION

OIOIIOOI OIIOIIIII OIIIOIOI OOIOOOOO OIIOOOOI OIIIOOIO OIIOOIOI OOIOOOOO OIIOOOOI OOIOOOOO
OIIOOOII OIIOIIOO OIIOOIOI OIIIIOIO OIIOOIOI OIIIOOIO OOIOOOOO OIIOOOII OIIOIIOO OIIOOIIII OIIOOOII OIIOOIII

33

ALIEN KNOWLEDGE 101

⚙ TECHNOLOGY

The Insectoid species uses hollow asteroids as interstellar "hive ships." As a hive ship has never been seen in our solar system, this schematic is based on Little Green Men records, which are sparse. Each hive ship can carry an estimated 1–2 billion drones. Hive ships are typically sent to a system to cleanse it of all "alien life" before a larger planetary ship arrives with the rest of the colony. Although considered one of the oldest species in the universe, the Insectoids favor a balance of technology and biology to meet their objectives.

Pods are designed for a one-way trip — to land the soldiers on a planet's surface

What's their speed?

OBSERVATION DOME

It's unlikely that the Insectoids use this area to enjoy views of the star-filled universe. Our current hypothesis is that it's some kind of galactic greenhouse – possibly to support the growing of the mold and fungus that's their primary food source.

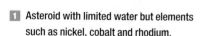

1. Asteroid with limited water but elements such as nickel, cobalt and rhodium.
2. Forward shield generators designed to protect the hive colony in deep space.
3. Drone launchers – when a hive ship enters a system, thousands of biomechanical drones are fired into space and at any nearby planets; it's these probes that alert the hive to the presence of life.
4. Glutinous mass – believed to be the ship's brain.
5. Drone launching pods – these small rock vessels are unpowered and fired towards their target.
6. Drone launching pod – typically has six drone warriors.
7. Breeding chambers – damp, moist caverns, covered with rotting fungus.
8. Maggot drones hatching.
9. Armory – designed to create weapons for individual Insectoid creatures, particularly the soldiers.
10. Bioengineering – much Insectoid technology is grown rather than built.
11. Ship's core.
12. Command center.
13. Fungal cavern (food store).
14. Observation dome.
15. Crystallized binary records chamber – each Insectoid hive ship seems to carry the entirety of Insectoid knowledge.
16. Propulsion system unknown – hyperspace capability estimated.

▶ THE SCIENCE OF BUGS

A SPECIAL REPORT BY SOO-JAN LEE

Any study of the Insectoid species can by definition only be theoretical as we've never seen any examples of the species and are reliant completely on intelligence from untrustworthy former allies. I should also emphasize that I have some reservations about the Insectoid outlines provided in this section – particularly the Insectoid brain – as they seem to have little substance in reality.

Firstly, let's be clear. We already live on an insect planet. There are over 900,000 different types of living insects in the world and they account for almost 90% of all the species on Earth. Our current estimate is that some 10 quintillion individual insects are alive at any one time. Relative to their size, insects are the strongest, fastest, and most poisonous life forms on Earth, and they have the most developed societies.

It's no surprise, therefore, that elsewhere in the universe insect life has developed instead of, for example, mammals or reptiles. One study has estimated that over 80% of the billions of species within the known universe are likely to be Insectoid in origin.

DEALING WITH INSECTOID ALIENS

▶ Insects don't think and feel the same way as other species. Their brains work completely differently and we have no reason to believe that this would change as the species advances.

▶ Insect races have probably developed specialized insect types to help them organize themselves efficiently. They'll be ruthless in their decision-making, thinking nothing of sacrificing billions of drones to protect the colony.

▶ Targeting the Queen would be a misguided tactic as there are frequently billions of female drones that can easily be developed into a new Queen. In addition, the Queen is likely to be at the center of the hive and therefore well protected.

INSECTS ARE THE GREAT ADAPTERS OF THE UNIVERSE AND THEORETICAL PROJECTIONS HINT THAT AT SOME POINT THE ENTIRE UNIVERSE WILL BECOME INSECTOID. IT'S POSSIBLE THAT SOME DIMENSIONS ARE ALREADY DOMINATED BY A SINGLE INSECTOID SPECIES THAT HAS ERADICATED ALL OTHER FORMS OF LIFE.

ALIEN KNOWLEDGE 101
ALIEN DISTRIBUTION

According to the mathematical modelling of Dr Soo Jan-Lee and her team, the universe is already Insectoid. The figures given here have been taken from an article entitled "The End of Carbon Chauvinism," which was published in *The American Journal of Astrobiology*, VXII, pages 920–922.

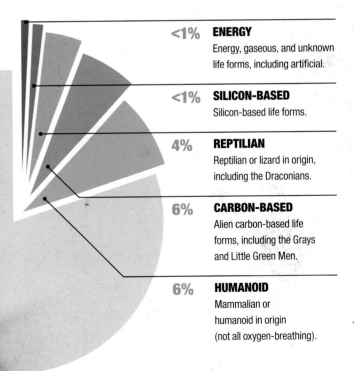

<1% **ENERGY**
Energy, gaseous, and unknown life forms, including artificial.

<1% **SILICON-BASED**
Silicon-based life forms.

4% **REPTILIAN**
Reptilian or lizard in origin, including the Draconians.

6% **CARBON-BASED**
Alien carbon-based life forms, including the Grays and Little Green Men.

6% **HUMANOID**
Mammalian or humanoid in origin (not all oxygen-breathing).

80% **INSECTOID**
Insectoid in origin, including arachnid and derived life forms.

NORDIC (MIRROR MAN, GLIMMER MAN)

The Nordics are a highly advanced species of inter-dimensional travellers who have visited Earth many times over the centuries. They can appear in different forms but most commonly they're seen as glowing, platinum-blond humanoids – hence the term "Nordic."

In some ways we know a great deal about the Nordics. We know that they travel throughout the universe, that they're opposed to violence of any kind, and that they have a keen interest in philosophy. In other ways we know very little. We don't know where they come from and we know nothing of the technology they use or why they've been coming to Earth for so many years.

The Nordics have never hidden their agenda; they just don't speak of it and refuse to be drawn in by human questioning. It's hard to tell exactly how many dimensional beings have visited our planet but there's certainly evidence of them throughout history. For example, the Anglo-Saxon Chronicles tell of a "light man" who appeared to King Harold in AD 1053.

ACCORDING TO THE NORDICS, THEY'RE PART OF A GROUP OF INTER-DIMENSIONAL SPECIES THAT HAVE ASCENDED FROM THE CURRENT UNIVERSE AND WHO NOW TRAVEL "EXISTENCE" GATHERING WISDOM AND KNOWLEDGE.

▶ APPEARANCE AND ABILITIES

WHAT WE KNOW!

Throughout history the Nordics have been known by many names, such as "Mirror Men" or "Glimmer People." They're humanoid in appearance but are said to have a distinct unearthly glow about them. Nordics have come in many forms over the years but seem to prefer the tall, fair, corporeal form that gives rise to their name.

Nordics seem unable to grasp some of the very real challenges we face on Earth, such as how to defend our planet. It may be that they've evolved so far that they're now unable to comprehend the vulnerability of less-developed creatures such as ourselves.

You really are perfect aren't you?

HEIGHT	6.5 feet (2 meters)
WEIGHT	Just right
COLOR	Glowing bronze
LIKES	Long, hypothetical conversations, Peter Gabriel's music
DISLIKES	Aggression, violence, and direct questions

PHYSICAL FEATURES

▶ Build is humanoid and muscular. Witnesses have encountered both male and female Nordics and it seems that the Nordics can adapt their form to ensure that humans are most comfortable in their presence.

▶ Their skin is a glowing bronze; some observers have referred to it as an "inhuman glow," free of blemishes.

▶ The Nordics appear to be ageless, supporting the theory that they appear in this form to present themselves more reassuringly to humanity.

▶

and with the apparent absence of any veins.

ABILITIES

▶ Nordics have a faint glow around them, perhaps due to the interdimensional nature of their travel. We suspect this to be residual energy from their dematerialization process.

▶ Nordics move slowly and deliberately. They can freely communicate in most languages of the world but are also adept at telepathy. They'll only enter a human's mind when the human has agreed to such a link.

▶ In their corporeal form, Nordics have similar strength and tolerances as a normal human, although they don't seem to feel cold or heat.

▶ Nordics can disappear or "evaporate" at will. A brief shining light appears behind them and they're gone.

MINISTRY OF ALIEN DEFENSE

ALIEN KNOWLEDGE 101
THE NORDIC AGENDA

This guy looks like a fifth member of ABBA

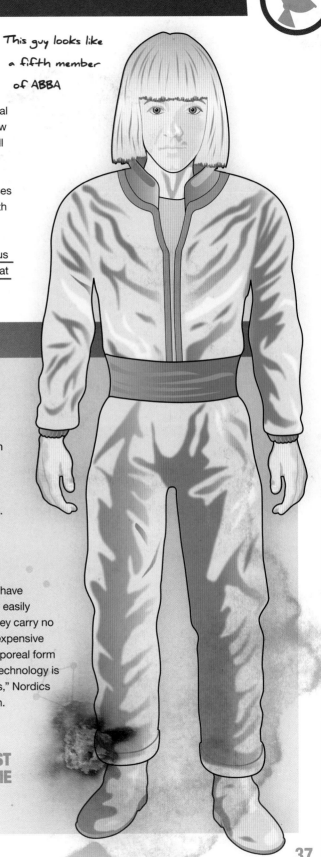

According to the Nordics, they're part of a group of interdimensional species that have ascended from the current universe and who now travel "existence" gathering wisdom and knowledge. It's hard to tell exactly how many so-called dimensional beings have visited our planet but there's certainly evidence for them throughout history. The Nordics are thought to be energy-beings who travel all universes searching for enlightenment. Needless to say, they don't get on with the Little Green Men. Their sharing comes not from offering their technology to humanity but their guidance and moral compass.

2/08 lm

One fear is that they're judging humanity and that if they deem us unworthy they could, with their immense power, not only ensure that we cease to exist but also that we never existed in the first place.

ALIEN MOTIVATION MATRIX: 1
OBSERVERS

Despite having god-like powers, the Nordics and other interdimensional light beings have never threatened or shown any interest in invading our planet. Their interest seems focused on the developing philosophies of humanity. They're unwilling to get involved in human affairs and avoid answering any questions that they deem unnecessary for human evolution. We believe that they know what will happen in the future but refuse to give us any clues.

ALIEN TECHNOLOGY MATRIX: T7
GOD-LIKE *"God Complex"*

Dimensional travel requires vast amounts of energy and as yet we have no idea how the Nordics generate this power or how they move so easily between dimensions. When they manifest themselves on Earth, they carry no technological equipment or special clothing. They may appear in expensive clothes or rags. But these are no illusions as they do appear in corporeal form and have been known to share meals with humans. Their level of technology is millions of years beyond our understanding. If referred to as "Gods," Nordics become visibly uncomfortable and are quick to deny this assertion.

WE'RE THE SAME AS PLANTS, AS TREES, AS HUMANS, AS THE RAIN THAT FALLS. WE CONSIST OF THAT WHICH IS AROUND US, WE'RE THE SAME AS EVERYTHING. IF WE DESTROY SOMETHING AROUND US, WE DESTROY OURSELVES.

TECHNOLOGY

The Nordics don't arrive on Earth in "ships" as we understand them. They appear via energy portal that they seem to be able to create at will. They carry no energy source and our theoretical understanding indicates that opening such a portal would require the energy of a small sun to complete. The Nordic species has clearly evolved beyond physical technology and somehow manages to harness the latent energy that's present everywhere in the universe. They carry no weapons or communication devices, although they seem to enjoy all forms of pocket watches and are fascinated by the clocks we have created on Earth.

Advances in our own knowledge of string theory and the quantum mechanics of the universe should bring us closer to understanding how Nordic technology functions, but as much of it's millions of years ahead of our own we're unlikely to grasp anything significant in the next few decades. The Nordics aren't a species we can rely on to share technology that could save Earth or help us to fight an alien invasion.

Interdimensional hypothesis not covered in my GCSE Physics course work — what are they hiding?

SOCIETY

We imagine Nordic society to be like a perfect hippie colony of the future – where arguments, aggression, and violence have been consigned to the history books. Nordics have been visitors to Earth throughout our recorded history and have always been patient and non-violent. They appear to have reached a pinnacle of "Zen" such that nothing can upset their balance. They appreciate philosophy, particularly Buddhism, to which they have a great affinity. They appear incapable of understanding humanity's penchant for violence and sometimes seem frustrated, even upset, by it.

> **THEIR RESPONSES TO QUESTIONS CAN BE OBTUSE AND INDIRECT, LEAVING THE HUMAN QUESTIONER UNSURE AS TO WHETHER THEIR QUESTION WAS ANSWERED OR NOT. THEY OFTEN REFER TO HUMANITY BEING "TESTED" AND ONLY RELUCTANTLY REVEAL INFORMATION ABOUT OTHER SPECIES IN THE UNIVERSE.**
> **MEN IN BLACK REPORT (AGENT MIB 997), LHASA, TIBET**

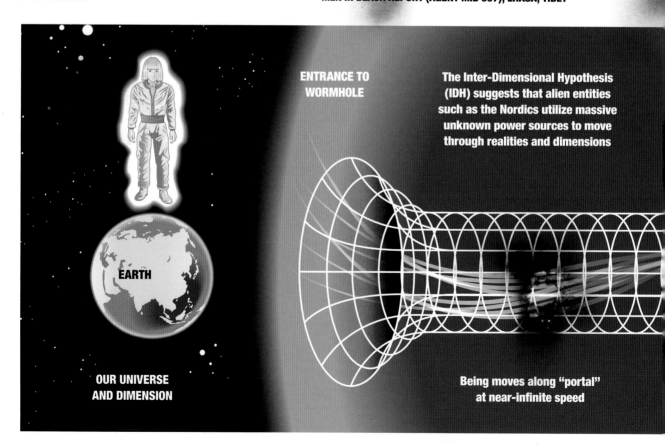

ENTRANCE TO WORMHOLE

The Inter-Dimensional Hypothesis (IDH) suggests that alien entities such as the Nordics utilize massive unknown power sources to move through realities and dimensions

EARTH

OUR UNIVERSE AND DIMENSION

Being moves along "portal" at near-infinite speed

> THEY MOVE ACROSS DIMENSIONS AND DO NOT REGARD SPACE OR TIME IN THE SAME WAY WE DO. IT COULD BE THAT THEY EXIST ONLY IN ENERGY FORM AND SO CAN EXIST EVERYWHERE AT THE SAME TIME.
>
> **DR JANE SORENSEN, HELSINKI INSTITUTE OF THEORETICAL SCIENCE**

ORIGIN AND HOME WORLD

Despite their human appearance, it's believed that the Nordics aren't revealing themselves in their real form. The only information ever released about their origin was to Tibetan monks. According to the monks, the Nordics inhabit what modern science refers to as the 10th Dimensional Reality – the sum of all universes and their outcomes.

One current line of investigation theorizes that the Nordics may in fact be humans from millions of years in the future who have perhaps returned to support our development. To date, the Nordics have resisted any attempts to have them share their knowledge of space travel with us and they won't be drawn into any discussion about whether they would support humanity if Earth were to be invaded.

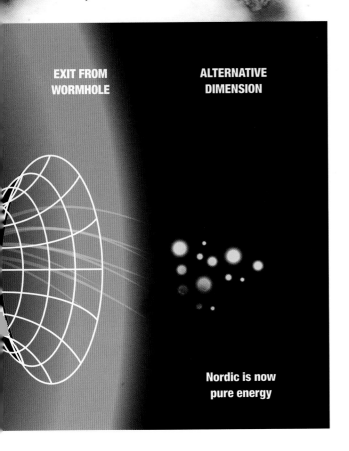

EXIT FROM WORMHOLE

ALTERNATIVE DIMENSION

Nordic is now pure energy

▶ SPECIAL CONTACT PROTOCOLS

MATERIALIZATION

History has shown that Nordics appear first as an apparition – often confused in the past as a "ghost." This is merely the first stage of their materialisation in this dimension. If they deem further exploration worthy, they typically follow up with a visit, appearing in the same location and slowly taking on a corporeal form.

A NON-VIOLENT FIRST RESPONSE

Don't try to hurl anything at the apparition. Never, ever attack a Nordic or other "light being" in its corporeal form. Don't wait for it to appear then think you're doing humanity a favor by trying to steal its "secrets." You won't harm it and, at best, the being will disappear and possibly never return. At worst, the interdimensional species may view us as unworthy of continued existence due to chronic violence, and destroy us all without us even knowing it.

BE PATIENT AND RESPECTFUL

As the being materializes from another dimension, wait patiently and then bow respectfully, but not in worship. Smile and hold up the palm of your hand in the universal sign of greeting.

SOME BACKGROUND MUSIC

Play suitable New Age music or some Stevie Nicks in the background. Conversation topics for Nordics include the joy of life and Zen philosophy or any Fleetwood Mac album apart from "Tusk." Ensure that the "aura" is kept calm and tranquil – these beings haven't expended the energy of our sun in crossing dimensions just to hear you say, "OMG, this is so totes amaze!"

CONSIDER YOUR RESPONSE CAREFULLY AND SPEAK SLOWLY AND CLEARLY – THE BEINGS MAY BE ASSESSING YOU AND YOUR INTELLECT. IF YOU ANSWER ANY QUESTION INCORRECTLY, NORDICS WILL OFTEN SAY TO YOU "THIS IS NOT CORRECT" – TO WHICH YOU SHOULD RESPOND, SOMEWHAT MYSTERIOUSLY "OR IS IT?," HINTING AT SOME DEEPER MEANING. ONLY USE THIS IF YOU REALLY HAVE TO "WING IT."

GLOSSARY

ABDUCTION To take someone away from a place by force.

BIOMATTER Plant material, vegetation, or agricultural waste used as a fuel or energy source; matter of biological origin; living or dead tissue.

CLONE A plant or animal that is grown from one cell of its parent and that has exactly the same genes as its parent; a person or thing that appears to be an exact copy of another person or thing.

COMPREHENSIVE Covering completely or broadly; inclusive; including many, most, or all things.

CONSPIRACY A secret plan made by two or more people to do something that is harmful or illegal; the act of secretly planning to do something that is harmful or illegal.

COVERT Made, shown, or done in a way that is not easily seen or noticed; secret or hidden.

CULT A small religious group that is not part of a larger and more accepted religion and that has beliefs regarded by many people as extreme or dangerous.

DEBUNK To show that something (such as a belief or theory) is not true; to show the falseness of (a story, idea, statement, etc.).

ECOSYSTEM Everything that exists in a particular environment; the complex of a community of organisms and its environment functioning as an ecological unit.

ELLIPTICAL Shaped like a flattened circle.

ERADICATE To remove (something) completely; to eliminate or destroy (something harmful).

EXTRATERRESTRIAL Coming from or existing outside the planet Earth; originating, existing, or occurring outside the earth or its atmosphere.

FRAGMENTARY Made up of parts or pieces; incomplete.

HYPOTHESIS An idea or theory that is not proven but that leads to further study or discussion; a tentative assumption made in order to draw out and test its logical or empirical consequences.

IMPLANT To put (something) in a specified place; to place (something) in a person's body by means of surgery; to cause (something) to become a part of the way a person thinks or feels.

INFRASTRUCTURE The basic equipment and structures (such as roads and bridges) that are needed for a country, region, or organization to function properly; the underlying foundation or basic framework (as of a system or organization); the permanent installations required for military purposes; the system of public works of a country, state, or region; the resources (as personnel, buildings, or equipment) required for an activity.

INTERGALACTIC Existing or occurring between galaxies; situated in or relating to the spaces between galaxies; of, relating to, or occurring in outer space.

INTERVENTION An interference with the outcome or course, especially of a condition or process (as to prevent harm or improve functioning).

MATRIX Something within or from which something else originates, develops, or takes form.

PHENOMENON Something (such as an interesting fact or event) that can be observed and studied and that typically is unusual or difficult to understand or explain fully; an observable fact or event; a fact or event of scientific interest susceptible to scientific description and explanation; a rare or significant fact or event; an exceptional, unusual, or abnormal thing or occurrence.

PHYSIOLOGY A branch of biology that deals with the functions and activities of life or of living matter (as organs, tissues, or cells) and of the physical and chemical phenomena involve; the organic processes and phenomena of an organism or any of its parts or of a particular bodily process.

RUDIMENTARY Basic or simple; not very developed or advanced; of a primitive kind.

SPECIES A class of individuals having common attributes and designated by a common name; a logical division of a genus or more comprehensive class; a category of biological classification ranking immediately below the genus or subgenus, comprising related organisms or populations potentially capable of interbreeding; an individual or kind belonging to a biological species.

STATISTIC A number that represents a piece of information (such as information about how often something is done, how common something is, etc.); a quantity (as the mean of a sample) that is computed from a sample.

THEORETICAL Relating to what is possible or imagined rather than to what is known to be true or real; relating to the general principles or ideas of a subject rather than the practical uses of those ideas; confined to theory or speculation often in contrast to practical applications; speculative and hypothetical.

VERIFY To confirm or substantiate in law by oath; to establish the truth, accuracy, or reality of something.

VIABLE Capable of working, functioning, or developing adequately; capable of being done or used; capable of succeeding.

FOR MORE INFORMATION

European Space Agency (ESA)
ESA HQ Mario-Nikis
8-10 rue Mario Nikis
75738 Paris Cedex 15
France
Tel: +33 1 53 69 76 54
Website: http://www.esa.int
The European Space Agency (ESA) is Europe's gateway to space. Its mission is to shape the development of
Europe's space capability and ensure that investment in space continues to deliver benefits to the citizens of
Europe and the world.

National Aeronautics and Space Administration (NASA)
NASA Headquarters
300 E Street SW, Suite 5R30
Washington, DC 20546
(202) 358-0001
Website: http://www.nasa.gov
NASA's vision: To reach for new heights and reveal the unknown for the benefit of humankind. To do that, thousands
of people have been working around the world—and off of it—for more than 50 years, trying to answer some
basic questions. What's out there in space? How do we get there? What will we find? What can we learn there,
or learn just by trying to get there, that will make life better here on Earth?

National Space Society
P.O. Box 98106
Washington, DC 20090-8106
(202) 429-1600
Website: http://www.nss.org
The National Space Society (NSS) is an independent, educational, grassroots, non-profit organization dedicated to
the creation of a spacefaring civilization. Its vision is people living and working in thriving communities beyond
the Earth, and the use of the vast resources of space for the dramatic betterment of humanity. Its mission to
promote social, economic, technological, and political change in order to expand civilization beyond Earth, to
settle space, and to use the resulting resources to build a hopeful and prosperous future for humanity.

SETI Institute (Search for Extraterrestrial Intelligence)
189 Bernardo Avenue, Suite 100
Mountain View, CA 94043
Website: http://www.seti.org

MINISTRY OF ALIEN DEFENSE

The SETI Institute's mission is to explore, understand, and explain the origin and nature of life in the universe, and to apply the knowledge gained to inspire and guide present and future generations. We have a passion for discovery, and for sharing knowledge as scientific ambassadors to the public, the press, and the government.

Space Foundation

4425 Arrowswest Drive

Colorado Springs, CO 80907

(719) 576-8000

(800) 691-4000

Website: https://www.spacefoundation.org

The Space Foundation's mission is to advance space-related endeavors to inspire, enable, and propel humanity. Founded in 1983, the Space Foundation is the foremost advocate for all sectors of space, and is a global, nonprofit leader in space awareness activities, educational programs, and major industry events.

Space Telescope Science Institute (STScI)

3700 San Martin Drive

Baltimore, MD 21218

(410) 338-4700

Website: http://www.stsci.edu/portal/

STScI is a free-standing science center, located on the campus of The Johns Hopkins University and operated by the Association of Universities for Research in Astronomy (AURA) for NASA. It operates the science program for the Hubble Space Telescope and will conduct the science and mission operations for the James Webb Space Telescope and supports other astronomy programs and conducts world-class scientific research.

SpaceX

Rocket Road

Hawthorne, CA

(310) 363-6000

Website: http://www.spacex.com

SpaceX designs, manufactures, and launches advanced rockets and spacecraft. The company was founded in 2002 to revolutionize space technology, with the ultimate goal of enabling people to live on other planets. It is the only private company ever to return a spacecraft from low-Earth orbit. In 2012, its Dragon spacecraft attached to the International Space Station, exchanged cargo payloads, and returned safely to Earth — a technically challenging feat previously accomplished only by governments. Since then Dragon has delivered cargo to and from the space station multiple times, providing regular cargo resupply missions for NASA. SpaceX will fly numerous cargo resupply missions to the ISS, and, in the near future, SpaceX will carry crew as well. Currently under development is the Falcon Heavy, which will be the world's most powerful rocket. All the while, SpaceX continues to work toward one of its key goals—developing reusable rockets, a feat that will transform space exploration by delivering highly reliable vehicles at radically reduced costs.

Websites

Because of the changing nature of internet links, Rosen Publishing has developed an online list of websites related to the subject of this book. This site is updated regularly. Please use this link to access this list:

http://www.rosenlinks.com/SACW/myths

FOR FURTHER READING

Aguilar, David A. *Alien Worlds: Your Guide to Extraterrestrial Life.* Des Moines, IL: National Geographic Children's Books, 2013.

Asimov, Isaac. *Extraterrestrial Civilizations.* New York, NY: Ballantine Books, 2011.

Brake, Mark. *Alien Life Imagined: Communicating the Science of Astrobiology.* New York, NY: Cambridge University Press, 2012.

Friedman, Stanton T. *UFOs: Real or Imagined?* (Haunted: Ghosts and the Paranormal). New York, NY: Rosen Publishing, 2011.

Friedman, Stanton T., and Kathleen Marden. *True Stories of Alien Abduction* (Off the Record!). New York, NY: Rosen Publishing, 2014.

Leivsson, Eirik. *UFOs and Aliens: Exceptional Cases of Alien Contact.* Seattle, WA: CreateSpace, 2016.

Petrikowski, Nicki Peter. *A New Frontier: The Past, Present, and Future Search for Extraterrestrial Life* (Search for Other Earths). New York, NY: Rosen Publishing, 2016).

Pye, Michael, and Kirsten Dalley. *Lost Cities and Forgotten Civilizations* (Mysteries Solved, Secrets Declassified). New York, NY: Rosen Publishing, 2012.

Scarsi, Andrea. *Extraterrestrial Channeling: Alien Abduction Syndrome.* Seattle, WA: CreateSpace, 2016.

Von Ward, Paul. *We've Never Been Alone: A History of Extraterrestrial Intervention.* Newburyport, MA: Hampton Roads Publishing, 2011.

Webb, Stuart. *Alien Encounters* (Paranormal Files). New York, NY: Rosen Publishing, 2012.

Webb, Stuart. *UFOs* (Paranormal Files). New York, NY: Rosen Publishing, 2012.

INDEX

Certificate in Alien Defense

This is to certify that

_____

has successfully completed all prescribed

requirements and is hereby designated a

Basic Level Alien Invasion Survivor

In testimony whereof, we have subscribed our signature

under the seal of the Ministry of Alien Defense

SPage

_____   _____
Ministry of Alien Defense   Signature Witness

MINISTRY OF ALIEN DEFENSE · DEFENDING EARTH FOR HUMANITY

AUTHOR'S ACKNOWLEDGEMENTS

I would like to dedicate this book to my daughter Nikita and wife
Constance, for whom I am working tirelessly to keep the Earth alien-
free. I also owe a big thanks to my partners in science fiction – Garry,
Steve and Tom, with whom I have spent many hours discussing various
alien-related matters over the years of our long friendship. A book
like this is never a solo project so I want to acknowledge the various
experts at the Ministry of Alien Defense I have driven insane with my
queries plus my contacts at NASA and Area 51. Finally, to my brother in
arms Richard for his patience and dedication to see through hours of
discussion, debate, and emails regarding everything from alien shield
technology to whether or not our Gray alien should have teeth. Also
to his Dad for his contribution on cattle abduction.

⚠ WARNING!

This book is a guide to resisting hostile alien forces but is not a
substitute for, nor should be relied upon as, professional instruction
by qualified personnel. The Ministry of Alien Defense and the publisher
disclaim, as far as the law allows, any liability arising directly or
indirectly from the use or misuse of the information contained in this
book. There is no guarantee that the preventative measures outlined
in this book will ensure that you are safe from abduction or cloning, or
that humanity can successfully resist an alien invasion. We would also
like to confirm that the author does not endorse or have commercial
links with any manufacturer or "brand" of aluminium tinfoil.